THE SCHOOLS HISTORY PROJECT

·S·H·P·

OFFICIAL TEXT

THE USA
BETWEEN THE WARS
1919–1941

a study in depth

**DISCOVERING
THE PAST
FOR GCSE**

Terry Fiehn

Rik Mills

Maggie Samuelson

Carol White

**Series Editor:
Colin Shephard**

HODDER
EDUCATION
AN HACHETTE UK COMPANY

© Terry Fiehn, Rik Mills, Maggie Samuelson, Carol White 1998

First published in 1998
by Hodder Education, an Hachette UK company
338 Euston Road
London NW1 3BH

Reprinted 1999, 2000, 2002 (twice), 2003, 2004, 2005, 2006, 2007,
2008 (twice), 2010, 2011

Layouts by Fiona Webb
Artwork by Mike Humphries, Linden Artists

Typeset in 10½/12 pt Walbaum Book by Wearset, Boldon,
Tyne and Wear

Printed and bound in Dubai
A catalogue entry for this title is available from the
British Library

ISBN 978 0 7195 5259 5
Teachers' Resource Book ISBN 978 0 7195 5260 1

Contents

The Schools History Project

Set up in 1972 to bring new life to history for students aged 13–16, the Schools History Project continues to play an innovatory role in secondary history education. From the start, SHP aimed to show how good history has an important contribution to make to the education of a young person. It does this by creating courses and materials which both respect the importance of up-to-date, well-researched history and provide enjoyable learning experiences for students.

Since 1978 the Project has been based at Trinity and All Saints University College, Leeds. It continues to support, inspire and challenge teachers through the annual conference, regional courses and website: *http://www.schoolshistoryproject.org.uk*. The Project is also closely involved with government bodies and awarding bodies in the planning of courses for Key Stage 3, GCSE and A level.

Enquiries about the *Discovering the Past* series should be addressed to the publishers, John Murray.

Series consultants
Terry Fiehn
Tim Lomas
Martin and Jenny Tucker

Note: The wording and sentence structure of some written sources have been adapted and simplified to make them accessible to all students, while faithfully preserving the sense of the original.

Words printed in SMALL CAPITALS are defined in the Glossary on pages 127–28.

Acknowledgements

Cover: Peter Newark's American Pictures; **p.2 and p.3** Courtesy Library of Congress; **p.4** *t* Corbis-Bettmann, *b* Peter Newark's American Pictures; **p.5** *t* Peter Newark's American Pictures, *b* Corbis-Bettmann/Underwood; **p.6** *t* Brown Brothers, *b* Corbis-Bettmann; **p.8** Corbis-Bettmann/UPI; **p.9** *l* Peter Newark's American Pictures, *r* Wiener Library; **p.10** *t* Corbis-Bettmann, *cl* Brown Brothers, *cr* Corbis Bettmann, *b* Peter Newark's American Pictures; **p.11** *tr* Courtesy George Eastman House, *tl* Brown Brothers, *b* Corbis-Bettmann/UPI; **p.14** *l* Peter Newark's American Pictures, *c and r* Corbis-Bettmann/UPI; **p.15** *l and r* Corbis-Bettmann/UPI; **p.18** *t* Courtesy Library of Congress, *b* Corbis-Bettmann; **p.19** *t* Corbis-Bettmann-Underwood, *b* Corbis-Bettmann; **p.21** *t* Ford Motor Company; **p.22** *l and r* Mary Evans Picture Library; **p.23** *tr* Corbis-Bettmann, *b* Courtesy George Eastman House; **p.24** *tr* Mary Evans Picture Library, *tl* Corbis-Bettmann, *b* Sears, Roebuck & Co.; **p.25** *l* Brown Brothers, *r* Corbis-Bettmann/UPI; **p.30** Ford Motor Company; **p.31** © Getty Images; **p.32** Ford Motor Company; **p.33** Peter Newark's American Pictures; **p.34** *t* © Getty Images, *b* Brown Brothers; **p.35** *t* Culver Pictures, *bl* Corbis-Bettmann, *br* Corbis-Bettmann/UPI; **p.36** *l* Corbis-Bettmann/UPI, *r* Corbis-Bettmann; **p.37** *t* Corbis-Bettmann/UPI, *b* Brown Brothers; **p.38** *l* Brown Brothers, *r* Famous Players/Paramount (courtesy Kobal Collection); **p.39** *t* Brown Brothers, *b* Equitable Life Insurance Company, New York/Bridgeman Art Library, London/New York © Estate of Thomas Hart Benton/VAGA, New York/DACS, London 1998; **p.40** *t* Corbis-Bettmann, *br* Brown Brothers, *bl* Corbis-Bettmann; **p.41** *t* © Getty Images, *b* Corbis-Bettmann/UPI; **p.42** Corbis-Bettmann/UPI; **p.47** *t* © Getty Images, *b* Corbis-Bettmann; **p.48** *l and r* Peter Newark's American Pictures; **p.50** *t* Courtesy Library of Congress, *b* Peter Newark's American Pictures; **p.52** Corbis-Bettmann/UPI; **p.53** Culver Pictures; **p.54** *l and r* Brown Brothers; **p.55** Corbis-Bettmann; **p.56** © Getty Images; **p.57 and p.58** Corbis-Bettmann; **p.59** Culver Pictures; **p.60** Corbis-Bettmann; **p.61** *tl and tr* Peter Newark's American Pictures, *b* Courtesy JC & H Productions; **p.62** *t* Courtesy Library of Congress, *b* Corbis-Bettmann; **p.63** Corbis-Bettmann; **p.64** Topham; **p.65** Peter Newark's American Pictures; **p.67** Corbis-Bettmann; **p.75** *tl* Popperfoto, *tr* Detroit News Archives, *b* Peter Newark's American Pictures; **p.76** *t and b* Corbis-Bettmann; **p.78** © Getty Images; **p.79** Corbis-Bettmann; **p.80** Culver Pictures; **p.81** Peter Newark's American Pictures; **p.82 and p.83** Culver Pictures; **p.84** Peter Newark's American Pictures; **p.85** Corbis-Bettmann; **p.86** Courtesy Library of Congress; **p.87** Corbis-Bettmann; **p.89** *t* Warner Bros (courtesy Kobal Collection), *b* Culver Pictures; **p.91** Culver Pictures; **p.92 and p.94** Corbis-Bettmann; **p.95** Corbis-Bettmann/UPI; **p.97** *l* Peter Newark's American Pictures, *r* Corbis-Bettmann/UPI; **p.99** *t* Mary Evans Picture Library, *b* Peter Newark's American Pictures; **p.101** *t and b* Corbis-Bettmann/UPI; **p.103** Peter Newark's American Pictures; **p.104** Corbis-Bettmann/UPI; **p.105** National Archives & Records Administration, Washington D.C; **p.106** *t* Corbis-Bettmann, *b* Brown Brothers; **p.107** *t* Brown Brothers, *cr* Culver Pictures, *cl* National Museum of American Art, Washington DC/Art Resource, NY, *b* Corbis-Bettmann/UPI; **p.110** *l* Peter Newark's American Pictures; **p.112** *l and r* Corbis-Bettmann; **p.115** *tl* Chicago Historical Society, *tr and b* Reproduced by permission of Punch Ltd; **p.118** Peter Newark's American Pictures; **p.119** Brown Brothers; **p.120** Corbis-Bettmann/UPI; **p.123** Brown Brothers; **p.124** Topham

(*t* = top, *b* = bottom, *r* = right, *l* = left, *c* = centre)

Every effort has been made to trace all the copyright holders, but if any have been inadvertently overlooked the publishers will be pleased to make the necessary arrangement at the first opportunity.

WAS THE USA THE LAND OF OPPORTUNITY?

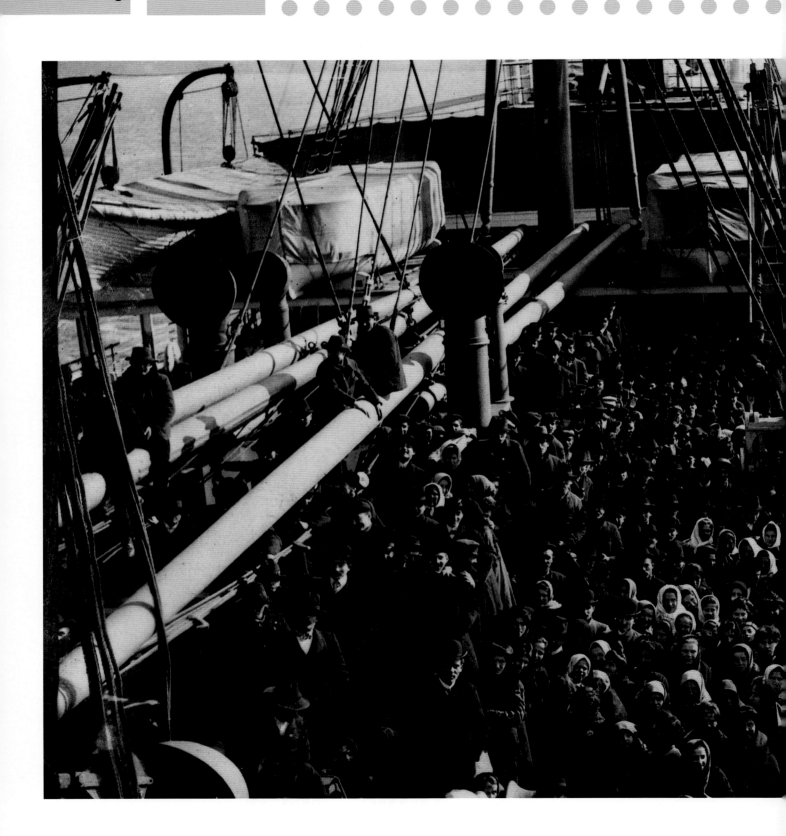

chapter 1

WHAT WAS LIFE LIKE IN THE LAND OF THE FREE?

Coming to America

BETWEEN 1850 AND 1914, over 40 million people (about 10 per cent of the population of Europe) left the Old World for America. It was a chance to start a new life in a country of golden opportunities. For most people, the two-week voyage to the USA was a hard one. They travelled in the cheapest class where the cramped conditions allowed little privacy. Rough weather, common on the Atlantic crossing, added to their misery.

So the IMMIGRANTS' first view of America, the Statue of Liberty, was a heartening one that marked the beginning of their new life. Or did it? First they had to pass through the immigration processing centre on Ellis Island – and there was no guarantee that they would get through.

SOURCE 1 Emigrants aboard the SS *Westernland*, c. 1890

SOURCE 2 Engraving of Jewish REFUGEES from Russia passing the Statue of Liberty, *Harper's Weekly*, 1892

SOURCE 3 Edward Corsi, *In the Shadow of Liberty*, 1935

66 *My first impressions of the New World will always be etched in my memory, particularly that hazy October morning (in 1907) ... The steamer, Florida, fourteen days out of Naples, filled to capacity with sixteen hundred natives of Italy, had weathered one of the worst storms in our captain's memory ... My mother, my stepfather, my brother Giuseppe, and my two sisters, Liberta and Helvetia, all of us together, happy we had come through the storm safely, clustered on the foredeck for fear of separation and looked in wonder on this miraculous land of our dreams ...*

Passengers all about us were crowding against the rail. Jabbered conversations, sharp cries, laughs and cheers – a steadily rising din filled the air. Mothers and fathers lifted up their babies so that they too could see the Statue of Liberty ... This symbol of America inspired awe in the hopeful immigrants. Many older persons among us, burdened with a thousand memories of what they were leaving behind, had been openly weeping ...

Directly in front of the Florida, half visible in the faintly-coloured haze, rose a second and even greater challenge to the imagination.

'Mountains!' I cried to Giuseppe. 'Look at them!'

'They're strange,' he said, 'why don't they have snow on them?'

He was craning his neck and standing on tiptoe to stare at the New York skyline.

Stepfather looked towards the skyscrapers, and, smiling, assured us that they were not mountains but buildings – 'the highest buildings in the world'. 99

The Isle of Tears

After their ship had docked, the immigrants, carrying their few belongings, were put on the ferry to Ellis Island where they were registered. With mixed feelings of excitement, fear and apprehension they waited in long queues to face a series of tests which would decide whether they were to be admitted or not.

It was the medical tests they feared most. Doctors looked for mental or physical abnormalities, marking immigrants' clothes with chalk: 'X' for mental illness, 'H' for heart and so on. Then the doctors checked for contagious diseases, such as trachoma – they used button hooks to lift up eyelids to check for this blinding disease. Anybody who was thought to have any illness was detained for days or sometimes weeks.

For those who did get through the first stage there were still more questions – about occupations, whether they could read or write and about their financial situation. Names were a problem as officials often could not understand them. Many immigrants ended up getting new names on their

SOURCE 4 A group of slavic immigrants being led upstairs to the Great Hall, 1905. Between 1900 and 1915, as many as 5000 immigrants arrived at Ellis Island every day

registration forms. One confused German Jew, when asked his name, said 'Ich vergesse' (I forget) and instantly became 'Ferguson' on his documents.

Many immigrants were detained for reasons other than illness. Young women on their own were held until relatives came for them. It was thought that a single woman might become destitute and turn to prostitution. Some immigrants had to wait for money from relatives before they were allowed to enter America.

SOURCE 5 The Great Hall at Ellis Island served as the main inspection hall

SOURCE 6 Public Health Service doctor examining an immigrant's eyes for trachoma at Ellis Island

Ellis Island was the end of the line for the old, ill and illiterate, and those who were seen as undesirable. They were sent back to Europe. In 1911 for instance, around two per cent were not allowed in. For them, Ellis Island was aptly named the 'Isle of Tears'.

But for the vast majority who passed the tests, it was down the grand staircase from the Great Hall, through the door marked 'Push to New York' and onto the ferry for Manhattan. There they could buy food and train tickets – railway agents could sell up to 25 tickets a minute on a busy day. Many immigrants still had long distances to travel before reaching their final destination in America. But their new life had begun.

■ TASK

Interview an Italian woman who came to the USA in 1912. You want to find out about Ellis Island, and what it was like to be an immigrant arriving in America. Write down your questions and what she says in reply. Some questions have been done for you, but you can add others of your own.

- How did you feel at the end of your journey?
- What were your feelings when you were taken to Ellis Island?
- What was it like in the Great Hall?
- What were the medical tests and registration questions like?
- What were your main hopes and fears for the future once you had been allowed in?

SOURCE 7 Angelo Pelligrini, Italian immigrant, talks about his family's stay on Ellis Island as they went through the tests for admission

" We lived there for three days – Mother and we five children, the youngest of whom was three years old. Because of the rigorous physical examination that we had to submit to, particularly of the eyes, there was terrible anxiety that one of us might be rejected. And if one of us was, what would the rest of the family do? My sister was indeed momentarily rejected; she had been so ill and had cried so much that her eyes were absolutely bloodshot, and Mother was told, 'Well, we can't let her in.' But fortunately Mother was an indomitable spirit and finally made them understand that if her child had a few hours' rest and a little bite to eat she would be all right. In the end we did get through. "

SOURCE 8 Immigrants who have successfully passed the admission tests, waiting to go to Manhattan. Between 1892 and 1924, Ellis Island handled 90 per cent of all immigrants arriving in the USA. Some people spent days on the island; others only a few hours before being allowed to leave for Manhattan

1. Why do you think the Americans insisted that immigrants were 'processed' through Ellis Island before being allowed in?
2. Why was Ellis Island called the 'Isle of Tears'?

Why did people want to come to 'the land of opportunity'?

THE IMMIGRANTS CAME from all over the world, but particularly from Europe. Most were young – in 1910 the average age in the USA was 24 – and eager to do well in their new country. Many were migrating because of factors 'pushing' them out of their own countries. But equally important, or even more important, were the factors 'pulling' them towards America. For these immigrants the USA seemed to be a land of great opportunity.

PULL FACTORS

Space
America had vast plains where farm settlements were miles apart. Growing cities had plenty of room around them to expand. By 1900 New York was the largest city in the world and still growing.

PUSH FACTORS

Overcrowding
Increases in population meant that many areas were overcrowded. There was a shortage of land and younger children in large families could not expect to inherit much when their parents died.

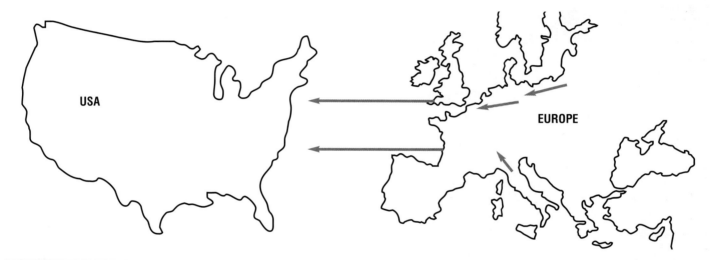

Natural resources
America had massive natural resources – oil, timber and minerals. Land was cheap.

Economic opportunity
American industry and business led the world. The USA had industrialised rapidly in the second part of the nineteenth century. The economy was still growing fast and employers needed a constant supply of labour. There were also good opportunities to set up new businesses.

Wages
Wages for skilled trades and those working in large factories were better than in Europe. A farm worker in the USA could expect to earn much more than he could in Europe and would be able to buy his own land.

The Land of the Free
Others wanted to go to America because they believed they would be free to practise their religion, and live their lives as they wanted, without interference. The American Bill of Rights (1791) had guaranteed freedom of religion, freedom of speech and freedom of the press.

Lack of opportunity
At the beginning of the twentieth century, Europe was still a class-dominated society. The upper classes owned the best land and housing and the upper-middle classes ran the businesses. It was difficult for an uneducated or poor person to improve their situation.

Unemployment
Many workers, skilled and unskilled, found themselves out of work towards the end of the nineteenth century. There were various reasons for this; for example, economic depression or the introduction of new machinery that had replaced workers.

Persecution
Many people were persecuted in their own countries, for political or religious reasons. For example, in the late nineteenth century, thousands of eastern European Jews faced persecution. 'POGROMS' or attacks were regularly carried out against Jews in Russia and other countries.

66 *Give me your tired, your poor,*
Your huddled masses yearning to breathe free
The wretched refuse of your teeming shore.
Send these, the homeless, tempest-tossed to me;
I lift my lamp beside the golden door. 99

SOURCE 1 The Statue of Liberty. Carved at the base of the statue was a poem by Emma Lazarus written in 1886

SOURCE 2 A Polish farm labourer, 1912

66 *I have a very great wish to go to America. I want to leave my native country because we are six children and we have very little land. My parents are still young, so it is difficult for us to live. Here in Poland one must work plenty and wages are very small, just enough to live, so I would like to go, in the name of our Lord God; perhaps I would earn more there.* 99

SOURCE 3 Edited extract from the Declaration of Independence, 1776

66 *We hold these truths to be self-evident, that all men are created equal, that they are endowed by their Creator with certain unalienable Rights, that among these are Life, Liberty and the Pursuit of Happiness.* 99

SOURCE 4 Louis Adamic, *Laughing in the Jungle*, 1932. Louis emigrated from Slovenia to the USA in 1913

66 *My notion of the United States was that it was a grand, amazing, somewhat fantastic place – the Golden country – huge beyond conception, untellably exciting.*
In America one could make pots of money in a short time, acquire immense holdings, wear a white collar and have polish on one's boots – and eat white bread, soup and meat on weekdays as well as on Sundays, even if one were but an ordinary workman to begin with.
I heard a returned Americanec [someone who had come back from the USA] tell of regions known as Texas and Oklahoma where single farms – ranches he called them – were larger than a whole province of Slovenia. In America even the common people were 'citizens' not 'subjects', as they were in the Austrian Empire and in most European countries. 99

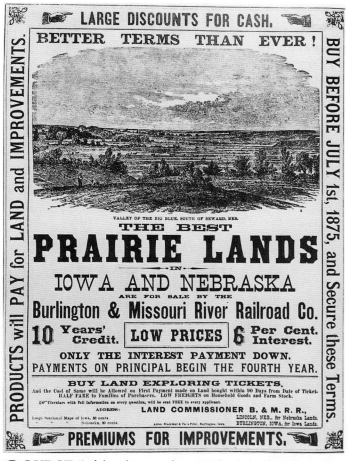

SOURCE 5 Advertisement for open lands in Nebraska, 1875

SOURCE 6 John Haug, son of a Norwegian immigrant

66 My father came from a really poor family. His father and grandfather were both tenant farmers in a little valley in a remote spot in Norway . . . It's a lovely place but the whole valley was owned by three people: the rest of the inhabitants were tenants and there was no chance whatever of getting ahead. 99

SOURCE 7 A German rancher, in the second half of the nineteenth century, said that America was much better than Germany

66 . . . because here I am free. In Germany I cannot say at all how I shall be governed. They govern the people with soldiers. They tried to make me a soldier too, but I ran away. 99

SOURCE 8 Pogrom victims in the Ukraine, 1918–20

■ TASK

1. Sources 1–8 show different reasons why immigrants moved to the USA. Draw a chart like the one below to show which of the sources demonstrate 'push' factors and which are 'pull' factors. Tick the relevant column (note that some sources may contain push and pull factors). In the final column explain why the source is a push or pull factor, or both. An example has been done for you.
2. Write a short piece describing why people wanted to emigrate to America. In particular, use the sources as examples or 'supporting evidence' of the points you are making.

Or

Draw a diagram to represent the key push/pull factors that made people want to emigrate to America. You can make this as imaginative as you like, including graphics.

Source	Push	Pull	Explanation
5		✓	Plenty of cheap land available. This pulled people to the USA.

Who were the Americans?

The melting pot

IMMIGRATION HAD MADE the USA a very mixed society. By 1920 there were 103 different nationalities living there. The motto on the Great Seal of the USA is *E pluribus unum* which means: 'From the many: one'. The idea was that America was like a melting pot, where immigrants lost their old identity and became Americans.

In practice, however, each new group of immigrants was treated with great suspicion by many of those who had already settled in America. They often got the worst jobs and the poorest pay. There was a definite hierarchy within American society. The white settlers who had arrived first dominated and the further back you could trace your ancestry the better!

SOURCE 1 The Great Seal of the USA

Old immigrants

The first European settlers came largely from northern and western Europe – particularly from Britain, Germany and Scandinavia. Their descendants tended to hold the best jobs, have the most money, and wield the most political power. They are sometimes called WASPS which stands for White Anglo-Saxon Protestants.

SOURCE 2 Wealthy, white Americans, 1900

SOURCE 4 A black family outside their home in Georgia, c. 1900

Native American Indians

Indians had originally lived across the whole of the North American continent. But they had been greatly affected by successive waves of immigration. Between 1850 and the 1890s they were gradually forced off their land. The last great battle between white settlers and Indian tribes was fought in 1895. By 1917 many Indians lived in a number of RESERVATIONS across America. Some tried to continue to live their traditional lifestyles as best they could, while others were assimilated into white society.

SOURCE 3 Indians from the Sioux tribe living on a government reservation in Dakota, c. 1900

Black Americans

In the eighteenth and nineteenth centuries millions of Africans were brought to America as slaves to work in the cotton plantations of the southern states. Slavery had been ended in 1865 after the Civil War. By 1920 there were 11 million black people living throughout America. Many worked as farmers or farm labourers in the old slave states of the South or as factory workers or labourers in the growing industrial cities of the North.

Southern and eastern Europeans

In the late nineteenth century most new immigrants came from eastern and southern Europe, particularly from Russia, Poland, and Italy. They were escaping persecution and poverty in Europe. Many of these 'new' immigrants were Jews and Catholics.

S**OURCE 5** Polish immigrants arriving at Ellis Island, c. 1900

S**OURCE 6** An immigrant woman and her children living in a tenement block in New York, c.1910

S**OURCE 7** A Chinese immigrant working as part of a railroad construction crew, 1885

Hispanics

The USA was as attractive to people from Central America, Mexico and South America as it was to those of Europe. The people from these countries were collectively known as Hispanics. They shared the common language of Spanish. Many Mexicans worked as cowboys on the great cattle ranches in the West.

Asians

Throughout the USA but particularly on the West Coast there was a growing number of Chinese and Japanese. The Chinese helped create the cities on the West Coast and many worked on the construction of the railroads.

1. Look at the photographs in Sources 2–7 on these pages.
a) What do they suggest about the different ways of life of the various groups?
b) Why do you think some of these groups might be unhappy about their life in America?
2. a) What do you think were the main problems in trying to achieve the motto on the American Great Seal (Source 1)?
b) What do you think the different ethnic groups might have come into conflict about?

How was the USA governed?

The Constitution

The USA was formed in 1787 after thirteen states had won independence from British control. They founded the Union and drew up a CONSTITUTION – a set of rules for how the country was to be governed. The Constitution still applies today. It can be changed by adding amendments if enough people agree.

The first ten amendments to the Constitution were called the Bill of Rights. They guaranteed freedom of religion; freedom of speech, and of the press; the right of people to meet peaceably together, and to petition the government. The Bill of Rights also gave citizens the right to carry weapons for self-defence, and to have a fair and proper trial.

A federal system

The USA has a federal system of government. This means that each state has its own government, but there is also a central government for the whole country. The central or FEDERAL GOVERNMENT of the USA is based in Washington DC. It has certain 'specified powers' over foreign policy, defence, trade, currency and the postal service. Other powers are kept by the individual states who can and do have different laws from each other.

Central government

The central government has three branches:

(1) President

The President of the USA combines the role of Head of the Government (like the British Prime Minister) and Head of State (like the British monarch). Unlike the British Prime Minister and monarch, the President is elected directly by the people. The President is also the Commander-in-Chief of the army and navy. He chooses advisers who are the heads of government departments.

The President is elected every four years.

(2) Congress

CONGRESS makes the laws. It also decides on taxation, and declares war or agrees peace. It can accept or reject the policies of a President. Like the British Parliament, Congress has two 'houses' – but both are elected. They are:

(3) Supreme Court

The SUPREME COURT has nine judges. They are not elected but are chosen by the President with the Senate's agreement. They make sure that the President and Congress obey the rules of the Constitution. They have to decide whether new laws are 'constitutional'.

House of Representatives	Senate
■ 435 'Congressmen' elected every two years.	■ 100 Senators elected for six years.
■ Each one represents about 450,000 voters.	■ Two senators come from each state – big or small.
■ States with the most people have the most Representatives.	■ One-third of the Senate are elected every two years.

Checks and balances

These three branches of government were created to work as a set of 'checks and balances' so that no single branch could become too powerful. For example, if Congress disapproves of the President's policies it can refuse to vote him the money to carry out these policies. But the President can veto laws passed by Congress. A two-thirds majority in Congress is needed then to overturn the President's veto. The Supreme Court can overrule them both.

The state governments

Each state government is also made up of three branches. These are: Governor, state legislature, state courts. State laws only apply to the state where they were passed. Federal laws apply to all states.

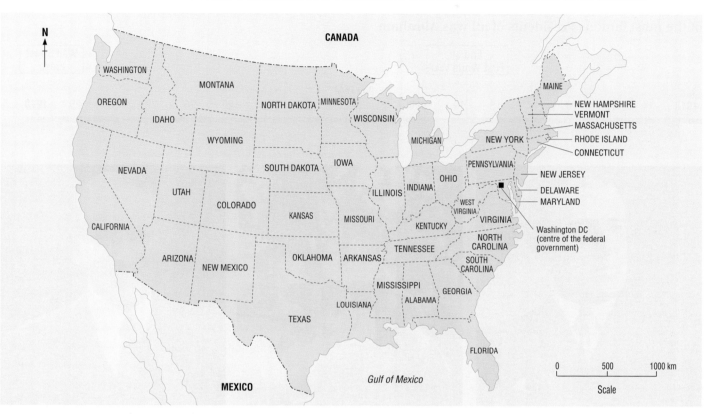

SOURCE 1 The original thirteen states in the Union had increased to 48 states by 1914. The USA today is made up of 50 states. (Alaska and Hawaii are not shown.)

Political parties

There are two main political parties in America: the REPUBLICANS and the DEMOCRATS. In the early part of the twentieth century the Republicans were seen as a conservative party. The Democrats were seen as a more progressive party.

The voters

The USA is a DEMOCRACY. Electors vote for the President, Congressmen, Senators, Governors and members of their state government. In some states they also vote for some public officials like judges.

Everyone over eighteen can vote. American women won the right to vote in 1920. The fifteenth amendment of 1870 gave voting rights to all citizens regardless of their race, colour, or religion. However, many states found a way round this. For example, Indians were not classed as citizens. Some states required a voter to be able to read. Others demanded that a person had lived in that particular state for a certain length of time before they were allowed to vote. In one state voters had to take an oath that they were not supporters of communism.

1. Say which of the following decisions would be taken by: Congress, the Supreme Court, the President.

Decision	Who would take it
To declare war	
To raise taxes	
To decide that a law is against the Constitution	

2. How might individual states be able to influence the policies of the central government?
3. It often happens that the President is a member of one political party but most of the Senators and Congressmen are from the other party.
a) What effect might this have on the government?
b) How could this weaken the President's power?
4. How does the Constitution try to stop the President from having too much power?
5. How does the American system of government try to protect the freedom of the people?

How could you become the President?

AMERICAN PRESIDENTS ARE extremely powerful despite the checks on their power built into the Constitution. They can affect the lives of every single American by the way they lead the country. So who the President is, is important.

In theory anyone could become the President. One of the most famous Presidents of all was Abraham Lincoln, who started life as the son of a poor farmer and worked his way up. Americans loved this sort of story: to them it was proof that America was the land of opportunity. In practice, however, in the twentieth century, there were certain qualities that helped you become President.

| Jan. 1913 | 14 | 15 | 16 | 17 WAR | 18 | 19 | 1920 | 21 | 22 BOOM | 23 | 24 | 25 | 26 | 27 | 28 | 29 | 1930 |

End of First World War

Wall Street crash

WOODROW WILSON 1856–1924
President: 1913–21
Born: Virginia
Father: church minister
Religion: Protestant
Job before election: university professor. Had no career in politics before he became President
Party: Democrat
Comments: clever, arrogant and stubborn. Wilson was a great crusader who thought the government should do more to tackle problems in America and around the world.

WARREN HARDING 1865–1923
President: 1921–23
Born: Ohio
Father: poor farmer/vet
Religion: Protestant
Job before election: newspaper owner and US Senator
Party: Republican
Comments: good socialiser and speaker. Harding got on well with people but was not clever or able. He liked girls and parties. He gave important jobs in the government to his friends from Ohio. Some of these were corrupt and took bribes, but Harding died before he could be involved in any scandal.

CALVIN COOLIDGE 1872–1933
President: 1923–29
Born: Vermont
Father: storekeeper
Religion: Protestant
Job before election: lawyer and Governor of New York, Harding's Vice President
Party: Republican
Comments: quiet and reserved, known as 'Silent Cal'. An honest and upright man, Coolidge believed that the best type of government was one that interfered least in the lives of its citizens. He did very little as President, and insisted on twelve hours sleep and an afternoon nap each day.

Should the government interfere?

One of the great dilemmas facing the President was how much the government should interfere in the lives of ordinary Americans or in the affairs of the states. The Founding Fathers, who drew up the Constitution, had intended that America be free of excessive government control. They wanted individuals to have as much freedom as possible. Some Presidents thought they should interfere very little in people's lives; others thought the government should interfere in order to help people in times of need and to protect the civil rights of individuals.

Start of New Deal								USA joins Second World War					

DEPRESSION and NEW DEAL | WAR

31 32 33 34 35 36 37 38 39 **1940** 41 42 43 44 **1945**

HERBERT HOOVER 1874–1964
President: 1929–33
Born: Iowa. Orphaned at eleven, grew up in Oregon
Religion: Protestant. Keen Quaker
Job before election: mine-owner, self-made millionaire and government minister for eight years
Party: Republican
Comments: very able administrator and organiser. Starting life as a poor orphan, he had made a fortune by the age of 40 – a 'rags to riches' story. He believed in 'RUGGED INDIVIDUALISM' – people succeeding by their own hard work and not relying on the government for help.

FRANKLIN D. ROOSEVELT 1882–1945
President: 1933–45
Born: New York State
Father: wealthy banker
Religion: Protestant
Job before election: lawyer and Governor of New York
Party: Democrat
Comments: from an old and established American family. His family had twelve ancestors on the *Mayflower* – the first ship to bring settlers from Britain to the USA. Worked extremely hard. He thought that government should take an active role and, if necessary, interfere in people's lives to prevent the rich benefiting at the expense of the poor.

1. Using the information provided, explain which of these qualities most helped someone become President and which helped least :

   ■ Catholic   ■ Jewish
   ■ white   ■ poor
   ■ Protestant   ■ rich
   ■ old   ■ black

2. Discuss how far governments should interfere in the lives of their citizens. You could draw up a list of the pros and cons of government interference in people's lives.

   We shall be coming back to this discussion throughout this book as it is a central issue and theme in the 1920s and 1930s in the USA.

chapter 2

HOW DID THE USA EMERGE FROM THE FIRST WORLD WAR?

THE USA HAD been reluctant to get involved in the First World War. Throughout the nineteenth century the USA's official policy was to isolate itself from European politics. It did not take sides in the disputes which affected Europe or get involved in alliances which might drag America into a war. Yet in 1917 the USA joined the war on the side of Britain and her Allies and made the deciding contribution that brought about the defeat of Germany and the Central Powers. However, the question that many Americans were asking in 1919 was: 'Was it worth it?'

Economic strength

The USA had come out of the war as the world's leading economy. The war had helped it in a number of ways:

- Throughout the war there had been a one-way trade with Europe. Money had poured into the USA for food, raw materials and munitions. American industry and agriculture had prospered.
- During the war the USA had taken over European overseas markets and many American industries had become more successful than their European competitors. For example, the USA had replaced Germany as the world's leading producer of fertilisers, dyes and other chemical products.
- The war had led to advances in technology; for example, mechanisation, and new materials like plastics. The USA was the world leader in developing these technological changes and applying them to industry.

1. Explain how the First World War helped the American economy – refer to the figures in Source 1.
2. Why do you think there were problems of unemployment after the war when industry seemed to be doing so well?
3. Why do you think the year 1919 might be called a 'year of crisis' in the USA?
4. Why do you think America went back to isolationism?
5. What point is the cartoonist making in Source 2?

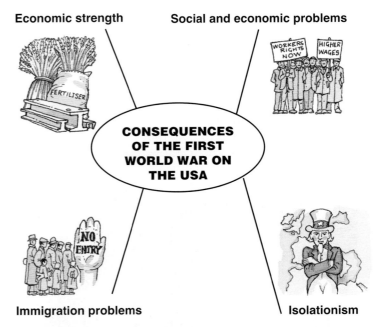

CONSEQUENCES OF THE FIRST WORLD WAR ON THE USA

Economic strength — Social and economic problems — Immigration problems — Isolationism

SOURCE 1 Statistics on production and exports between 1914 and 1917

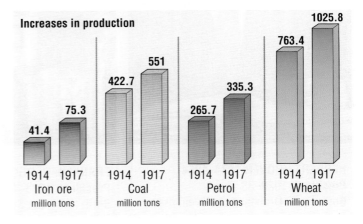

Increases in production

	1914	1917
Iron ore (million tons)	41.4	75.3
Coal (million tons)	422.7	551
Petrol (million tons)	265.7	335.3
Wheat (million tons)	763.4	1025.8

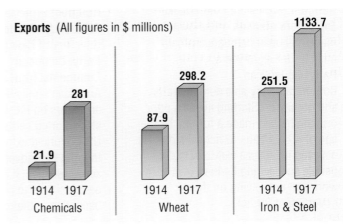

Exports (All figures in $ millions)

	1914	1917
Chemicals	21.9	281
Wheat	87.9	298.2
Iron & Steel	251.5	1133.7

Social and economic problems

Unemployment and strikes

Four million soldiers were demobbed in 1919. At the same time, industries, geared up to high levels of production during the war, laid off workers so returning soldiers were lucky to find employment. There was more trouble on the work front. Prices had doubled between 1914 and 1919 but wages had hardly risen at all. Workers demanded higher wages but bosses knew that high unemployment gave them a strong hand, and were unwilling to compromise. The result was a wave of violent strikes, which went on throughout 1919.

Fears of radicalism

In Europe the war had triggered the Communist revolution in Russia. And in the USA, the home of capitalism, two Communist parties were established in 1919. ANARCHISTS started a wave of bomb attacks.

The rise of Communism combined with the violent strikes by workers, made people terrified that revolution was spreading to the USA.

Race riots

In 23 cities across the USA, there were race riots in 1919. Many black people, who had moved to the northern cities from the South after 1910, found themselves under attack from the white communities around them. These riots were also a reaction to the discrimination and poor economic circumstances that blacks faced after the war.

Isolationism

President Woodrow Wilson was expecting the USA to take a leading role in world affairs after the war. He had drawn up the 'Fourteen Points' which became the basis for the newly created League of Nations. He desperately wanted the USA to play a major part in the League and thus achieve his dream of world peace.

But in 1919 the mood in the USA was against the League and against Wilson. Many thought America had already done more than enough in the First World War. Americans did not want their soldiers to be killed trying to resolve disputes around the globe. They were afraid that the USA would end up paying the bill for European squabbles. The vast majority of Americans wanted to return to the ISOLATIONISM of the nineteenth century.

In 1919 and 1920 Congress refused to support Wilson and rejected the League. Shortly afterwards they rejected Wilson himself. They voted for what the new Republican President Harding called 'normalcy'. Harding had invented this word and no-one at the time knew exactly what he meant. But it was a powerful idea. Americans wanted to get back to normal – to what life had been like before the shock of the war.

SOURCE 2 A cartoon from the *San Francisco Chronicle*, which shows President Wilson's struggle with Congress over whether America should join the League of Nations

Immigration problems

For some Americans these feelings of isolationism went even further. They wanted to end the open-door policy that had brought millions of people to the USA in the nineteenth century.

Attitudes to immigrants had been changing for some time. By 1900 there was not as much land available and, as industry became more mechanised, the need for workers declined. Also, Americans believed that the quality of immigrants was declining – many of the newer immigrants were poor labourers with little formal education.

Anti-immigrant feeling had increased during the war, especially against Germans. In 1917 a literacy test meant that immigrants had to prove they could read a 40-word passage before they would be allowed into America. These tests disadvantaged people from eastern Europe, Italy, and Russia as many of them had not been to school.

After the war, problems for new immigrants in the post-war depression got worse. Immigrant GHETTOS were appearing in the big northern cities of America. They were often dangerous places with violent crime, drunkenness, and prostitution. Many Americans believed the immigrants were to blame for these urban problems. This led to a widespread intolerance of foreigners which continued into the 1920s.

6. How does Source 4 explain American attitudes to immigrants and fears of radicalism?
7. Make a list of the problems facing the USA at the beginning of the 1920s.

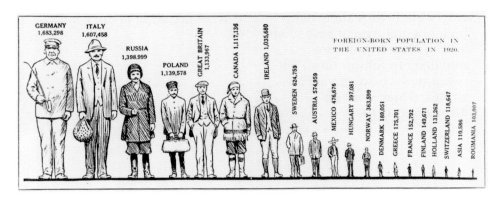

SOURCE 3 Foreign-born population of America in the 1920s

SOURCE 4 A cartoon from 1891, showing immigrants bringing problems into the USA. The judge is saying to Uncle Sam, 'If immigration was properly restricted, you would no longer be troubled with anarchy, socialism, the Mafia and such kindred evils'.

THE USA IN THE 1920s: WAS THIS A GOOD TIME FOR ALL?

The 1920s was a decade of extremes. On the one hand there was a booming economy which made cheap, mass-produced consumer goods available to people in a way that they had never been before. It was the age of the car and mass-entertainment – radio, cinema, dancing, jazz music and sport – which brought major changes in the American way of life.

On the other hand, not far below this surface prosperity lay poverty, intolerance and violence. The 1920s saw PROHIBITION, the rise of crime by gangsters and the growth of the Ku Klux Klan. Changes in industry and the introduction of new technologies left many Americans in a poverty trap from which they could not escape. In the land of plentiful food, farmers could not earn enough to support their families.

In this section you will look at both sides of American life and investigate which groups found the 1920s a time of prosperity and indulgence, and which groups found it a decade of poverty and intolerance.

chapter 3

TO WHAT EXTENT DID THE AMERICAN ECONOMY BOOM IN THE 1920s?

The richest country in the world!

AFTER A SHORT POST-WAR depression the American economy grew rapidly in the early 1920s. In 1926 the government announced that the standard of living in the USA was the highest it had ever been in the country's history. Americans were officially the richest people in the world!

This 'feel-good' factor made people confident about American success. It seemed that businessmen could do nothing wrong. Americans talked about prosperity with a capital 'P' as if it was a religion – everyone had a right to be prosperous. If you worked hard then you could be successful.

But what did this boom amount to? Did every part of the economy boom? Did all Americans benefit from it?

SOURCE 1 Andre Siegfried, a French writer, in *America comes of Age*, 1927

66 *European luxuries are often necessities in America. One could feed a whole country in the Old World on what America wastes. American ideas of extravagance, comfort and frugality are entirely different from European. In America the daily life of the majority is on a scale that is reserved for the privileged classes anywhere else. To the American, Europe is a land of paupers, and Asia a continent of starving wretches.* 99

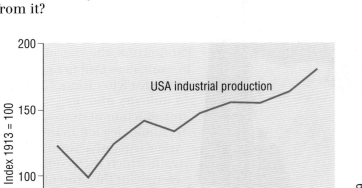

SOURCE 2 Graph showing the rise in industrial production and Gross National Product 1920–29

SOURCE 3 Number of millionaires

1914: 7000
1928: 35,000

1. What evidence can you find in Sources 1–5 to justify the claim that there was a boom in the American economy in the 1920s?
2. Who, according to these sources, seems to be doing very well in this period?

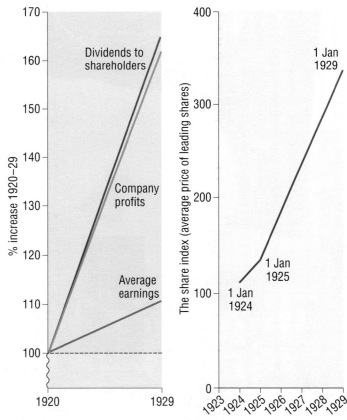

SOURCE 4 The graph on the left shows the rise in company dividends and company profits 1920–29. The graph on the right shows the value of stocks on the Wall Street Stock Exchange 1923–29

SOURCE 5 A street lined with cars (mostly Model Ts) in a town in Texas, c. 1920. Thousands of ordinary Americans had cars in the 1920s when they were still a privilege of the rich in Europe

Numbers represent percentage of civilian labour force

SOURCE 6 Graph showing unemployment 1920–29

3. Does Source 6 support the idea that everybody was doing well in the 1920s?
4. What is happening to average wages in Source 4 while company profits soar?
5. a) What do you think is the message of the cartoon in Source 7?
   b) What evidence can you find in the other sources to support this view?

SOURCE 7 A 1920s cartoon

In what ways did the American economy boom?

New industries

The boom was dominated by the so-called 'new' industries: cars, chemicals, electricity and electrical products. Cars led the way. Mass-produced cars were so cheap that most Americans were able to afford them. The enormous increase in the number of cars created a demand for steel, glass and rubber, so these industries also boomed. The American chemical industry led the world in products like fertilisers and dyes, but was also producing new plastics and man-made fibres that had a wide range of uses.

Electricity had developed slowly before the war but in the 1920s the electrical industry really boomed. By 1929 most homes in the cities had electricity and nearly 70 per cent of all Americans had electric lights. Factories were increasingly run by electricity. The amount of electricity consumed doubled in the 1920s. The electrification of America led to the development of a whole range of domestic goods – cookers, refrigerators, vacuum cleaners, washing machines and radios. These were new industries that had not existed on any kind of scale before.

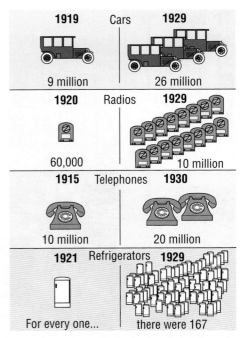

SOURCE 1 A chart showing sales of consumer goods 1914–30. Consumer goods were a major growth area in the 1920s. In the years before 1914 average annual sales were just above $4 billion; in the 1920s, they were above $7 billion

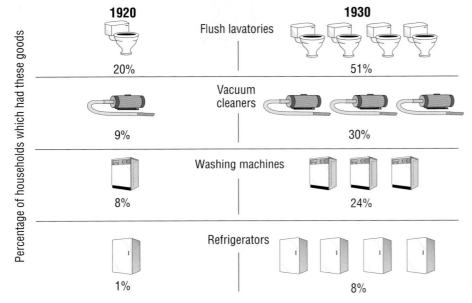

SOURCE 2 A chart showing how consumer industries boomed between 1920 and 1930

SOURCE 3 An advertisement for an electrical water heater from the 1920s

1. Which industries were growing fastest in the 1920s?
2. How did the development of new materials and new technology affect American industry?
3. Sources 1–4 show a range of products. Choose three of these products and explain how people's lives would have been changed by them.

SOURCE 4 An advertisement for a vacuum cleaner from the 1920s

Transport

During the 1920s the American transport system saw massive improvements. By 1930 the miles of paved road had doubled. It was not only the increasing number of cars that used these roads. The number of trucks had tripled to 3.5 million by 1929. The number of buses also increased, taking away passengers from the railways. Aircraft for civil flights made their first appearance in the 1920s, making 162,000 flights by 1929.

SOURCE 6 Passengers boarding a Boeing 40B-4, belonging to Pacific Air Transport, c. 1927

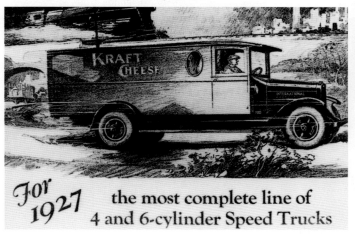

For 1927 the most complete line of 4 and 6-cylinder Speed Trucks

SOURCE 5 The illustration from an advertisement for an international truck company, 1927

SOURCE 7 Cherokee Indians working on the construction of the Empire State Building. Announced in 1929, it was to be the tallest building in the world

Construction

The American construction industry was busier in the 1920s than it had ever been before. Industrial growth created a demand for new factories. There was a boom in office building as the number of banks, insurance and advertising companies, and showrooms for cars and new electrical products, grew rapidly. Even more people were employed in building roads to serve the ever-increasing number of cars.

This was the age of the skyscraper. As confidence in America soared, the big companies sought to demonstrate their power and prestige by creating ever taller and grander buildings. The great growth in wealth also saw the construction of hospitals, schools and other public buildings.

Advertising

A whole advertising industry grew up to promote the vast range of consumer goods on offer. It used increasingly sophisticated techniques: adverts were more colourful than before and catch-phrases were introduced. Magazine advertising increased greatly and radio advertising began as a completely new venture.

Shopping

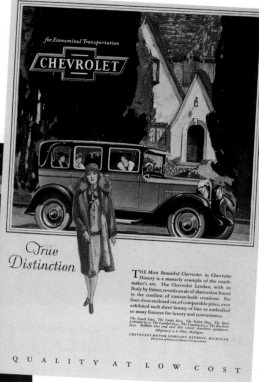

SOURCE 8 An advertisement for a Chevrolet Landau, 1927

SOURCE 9 The inside of Bloomingdales, a large chain store in New York

In the cities, chain-stores opened to stock the new range of goods now available. It was at this time that clothing for women started to be mass-produced. Manufacturers realised that certain dress sizes could be made which would fit most of the women in the country; there was a much wider choice of materials and styles than ever before. Clothing sales went up 427 per cent in the 1920s.

The improving truck industry and road system meant that goods could be delivered more easily by mail order. People living in remote, country areas could buy anything from farm machinery to frying pans and denim jeans. The number of mail-order companies grew enormously. The most famous of these was Sears, Roebuck and Co. of Chicago. In 1928 nearly one-third of Americans bought goods from the company – giving it sales worth $347 million that year.

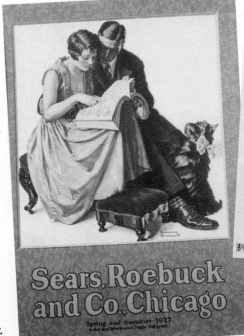

SOURCE 10 The cover of Sears, Roebuck and Co. mail order catalogue, 1927

SOURCE 11 Advertisement for rayon stockings.Silk stockings were a luxury item. In the 1920s rayon was invented which was a cheaper alternative to silk. In 1930 300 million pairs of rayon stockings were sold

Entertainment

Newspapers and magazines

The circulation of newspapers and magazines expanded enormously in the 1920s. In 1919 the first tabloid newspaper, the *Daily News*, had been published. This was followed by many others specialising in crime stories, strip-cartoons and national disasters. There were far fewer serious articles – most space was given to sports, fashion and movie stars. In 1922 ten magazines claimed a circulation of over 2.5 million.

Sport

Increasing affluence and leisure time saw the growth of spectator sports. In 1924 it was reported that 67,000 people watched the football match between Illinois and Michigan at the Memorial Stadium. In 1926 some 145,000 saw the boxing match between Jack Dempsey and Gene Tunney. But baseball was the most popular game, and its most celebrated star was Babe Ruth. Sport was a profitable business and millions of dollars changed hands.

SOURCE 12 A baseball game at a stadium in New York

Cinema

By the 1920s Hollywood had become the film-making capital of the world and movie-going had become one of the most popular leisure pursuits in America. In 1920 there had been 40 million cinema tickets sold each week. By 1930 it was nearer 100 million. There was a so-called 'picture palace' in almost every town.

Film-making became a MASS-PRODUCTION industry, with three films rolling off the Hollywood production line each week. Comedies were the most popular: they were made quickly and had a standard formula so that viewers knew what to expect. All these early films were silent; 'talkies' arrived at the end of the 1920s.

The Birth of a Nation became the first blockbuster movie and made $60 million dollars profit for the studio. The stars of the 1920s became household names and everybody wanted to read about them in magazines.

SOURCE 13 Charlie Chaplin in a film called *The Kid*. In 1917 Chaplin, 28 years old, signed Hollywood's first $1 million contract to star in eight films. He had become popular all over the world

4. How do you think the way that America 'looked' had changed by the end of the 1920s? Mention:

   ■ what you would have noticed about the streets and buildings (and what was on them) in the towns and cities

   ■ what you would have seen as you travelled around the countryside.

■ TASK

Draw a chart showing the main features of the economic boom of the 1920s. Show how many of these were linked.

■ DISCUSSION

America was now a 'consumer society'. What do we mean by this?

Resources

The USA had a great store of natural resources such as wood, iron, coal, minerals, oil and land. These had helped America to become a great industrial power by the beginning of the twentieth century, and provided a sound basis for further expansion in the 1920s.

Impact of First World War

The USA had come out of the war well (see page 16). It had supplied Europe with many goods during the war and had taken over European overseas markets. In some areas, US industry was now the world leader, e.g. chemicals. The war hastened technological change (see below) which US industry seized on.

Technological change

This was a period of great innovation. Plastics like Bakelite were developed effectively for the first time and were used in new household products. There were technological developments in many areas – automatic switchboards, glass tubing, conveyor belts, and concrete mixers. These helped modernise existing industries and develop new ones.

Underpinning all these changes was the development of electricity. Electricity provided a cheaper, more efficient source of power for factories. It also led to the production of new consumer goods such as refrigerators, vacuum cleaners and radios.

ALL OF THESE factors fed into the boom. Once it started, the boom became self-generating. The mass-production of cars stimulated the growth of industries that produced parts for cars: tyres, glass, metal and so on. More cars also led to the building of more roads and service stations, and an increased consumption of petrol. The development of electricity stimulated the growth of new industries making electrical products. New companies, setting up offices and large stores, created a demand for more buildings, so helping the construction industry. More people employed and earning a decent wage meant an increasing demand for goods.

Mass-production

New techniques meant that goods could be produced much more cheaply on a large scale. Henry Ford had pioneered mass-production in the car industry by introducing an assembly line (see page 30) before the war. He made cars so cheaply that thousands of ordinary Americans could afford them. In the 1920s, his ideas were applied throughout industry, particularly to the new consumer products.

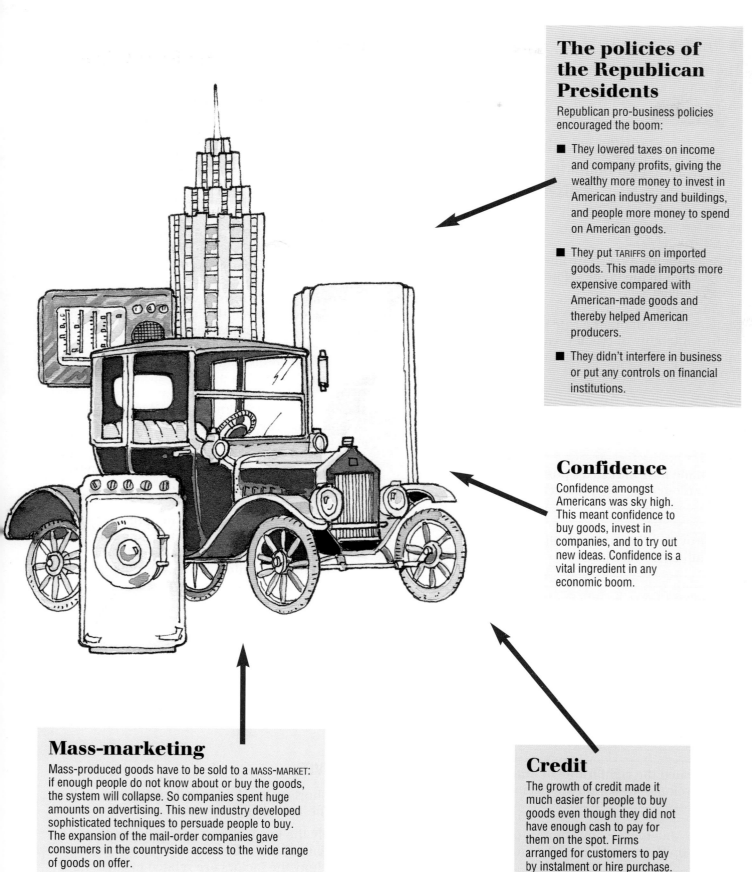

The policies of the Republican Presidents

Republican pro-business policies encouraged the boom:

- They lowered taxes on income and company profits, giving the wealthy more money to invest in American industry and buildings, and people more money to spend on American goods.

- They put TARIFFS on imported goods. This made imports more expensive compared with American-made goods and thereby helped American producers.

- They didn't interfere in business or put any controls on financial institutions.

Confidence

Confidence amongst Americans was sky high. This meant confidence to buy goods, invest in companies, and to try out new ideas. Confidence is a vital ingredient in any economic boom.

Mass-marketing

Mass-produced goods have to be sold to a MASS-MARKET: if enough people do not know about or buy the goods, the system will collapse. So companies spent huge amounts on advertising. This new industry developed sophisticated techniques to persuade people to buy. The expansion of the mail-order companies gave consumers in the countryside access to the wide range of goods on offer.

Credit

The growth of credit made it much easier for people to buy goods even though they did not have enough cash to pay for them on the spot. Firms arranged for customers to pay by instalment or hire purchase.

■ TASK

The diagram below shows the factors which caused the boom.

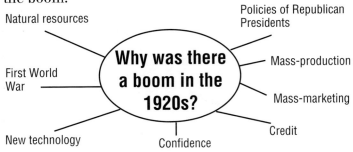

Natural resources

Policies of Republican Presidents

Why was there a boom in the 1920s?

First World War

Mass-production

Mass-marketing

New technology

Confidence

Credit

The statements A–H show how these factors contributed to the boom. Match them with the correct factor.

For example:

Statement A is about the role of 'credit' in the boom – the availability of credit meant that people could buy products even if they did not have enough money.

A meant people could buy products even if they did not have enough money

B made new industries possible and helped to modernise old industries

C provided the materials the growing industries required

D meant more people could afford to buy cars and other goods

E gave American industry a flying start at the beginning of the 1920s

F encouraged people to buy many more products

G created the right frame of mind in which developments could take place

H gave businesses the chance to expand without government restrictions

The policies of the Republican Presidents

The boom of the 1920s took place while the Republican Party was governing the USA. From 1921 to 1929 all the Presidents were Republicans and their party also controlled Congress. The Republicans were pro-business: they believed that it was the right of every American to seek prosperity. They believed that what was good for business was good for America. 'The business of America is business,' said President Calvin Coolidge, and on another occasion: 'The man who builds a factory builds a temple. The man who works there, worships there.'

Republican policies (see page 27) can be summed up in the term 'LAISSEZ FAIRE'. The Republicans believed that if you left businesses alone, they would make money and create jobs which would benefit all Americans. The government could help most, they thought, by interfering as little as possible.

The Republicans believed that it was this spirit of free enterprise that had made America great. Just 50 years earlier much of the country had been a wilderness. Americans had tamed it and developed it by their 'rugged individualism'; they had achieved success through their own efforts – this was the American way.

1. Why are the policies of the Rebublican Presidents called 'laissez-faire' policies?
2. Why did the Rebublicans believe that the government should not interfere in business?
3. What do you understand by the term 'rugged individualism'?

■ ACTIVITY

Write a short essay: Why was there a boom in the USA in the 1920s? In your essay:

■ identify the key factors and show how they contributed to the boom
■ show how the factors are related to each other
■ pick out the three factors you think were most important.

How did Henry Ford make the Ford Motor Company the most successful in the world in the 1920s?

1 Henry Ford's parents were farmers near Detroit. They wanted Henry to be a farmer too, but he had other plans. Henry was more interested in making tools and machines.

2

Ford wanted to make his own 'horseless carriage'. He read about petrol engines in a science magazine and in 1896 he made his first vehicle.

3 In 1899 Ford became superintendent of the Detroit Automobile Company. He built twenty cars in two years but the company failed because other firms made sturdier and simpler cars. Ford was bitterly disappointed. He did not intend to fail again.

Soon I will have enough money to open my own company.

Ford built a powerful but lightweight racing car. When he began to win races, it gave him the reputation he needed to raise money to start his own firm.

4

1903: The Henry Ford Motor Company is born. This time Ford did not fail. In five years he successfully made and sold eight different models. His factory expanded five-fold and he was building 100 cars a day.

5 In 1911 Ford announced that he would make a car for the ordinary man, not a big car, but large enough for a family. It was to be built from the best materials using new mass-production methods. It would be cheap to buy and to run. He called it the Model T.

One minute to make a whole car!

6

The Model T was the right product at the right price at the right time. It was a very basic car. You could have only one colour – black. But it was sturdy, extremely reliable and built with interchangeable parts. The Model T was a phenomenal success. In its first year 10,000 were sold. By the mid-1920s one out of every two cars sold was a Model T, and Ford was fabulously wealthy.

Why is Henry Ford so significant in American history?

HENRY FORD WAS much more than simply a car manufacturer. He came to symbolise the spirit of business enterprise in the 1920s. He was more famous than most presidents; people recognised his name because it was on so many cars. He had a major impact on American society.

Mass-production

Ford pioneered a totally new method of making cars. Parts were added to the car as it travelled along an assembly line. The worker fitted the component for which he was responsible – a headlight, a door, an engine – as the car passed by him. The most difficult work was done by machines. The Ford factory in Detroit was producing one car every three minutes in 1913. By the 1920s, a car was turned out every ten seconds. These mass-production techniques were taken up by other industries in America, which led to the production of masses of cheap goods which could be afforded by thousands of ordinary Americans.

SOURCE 1 The Ford assembly line in operation

SOURCE 2 Henry Ford, speaking to S. Crowther in *Today and Tomorrow*, published in 1926

❝ The work is planned on the drawing board and the operations sub-divided so that each man and each machine do only one thing . . .

The thing is to keep everything in motion and take the work to the man and not the man to the work . . . The men do not leave their work to get tools – new tools are brought to them . . . ❞

1. Use Sources 1–3 to explain how Ford's mass-production system worked.
2. What were the advantages of the assembly line?

SOURCE 3 A writer describing the Model T assembly line

❝ In the assembling plant everyone works 'on the belt'. This is a big steel conveyor, a kind of moving sidewalk, waist-high. It is a great river running down through the plant. Various streams come into the main stream, the main belt. They bring tyres, they bring headlights, horns, bumpers for cars. They flow into the main stream.

It is a belt. The belt is boss. It moves always forward. Now the chassis goes on the belt. A hoist lifts it up and places it just so . . . The chassis is deposited on the belt and it begins to move. ❞

Business ideas

Many people tried to copy the business ideas of the richest man in America. Ford's autobiography, which gave tips on how to succeed, was a bestseller in twelve languages. Ford believed in hard work, for himself and his workers. Every day he walked miles around his factory, making sure that workers were doing their jobs properly; he insisted that the cars were well built and that there was no shoddy workmanship. He was also constantly on the look out for ways of improving and speeding up the production process.

One big problem for Ford was that his workers were leaving after only a few months because the work was so monotonous and exhausting. So, in 1914, Ford announced that he was going to double the daily wage to $5. This was much more than anybody else paid and workers flocked to Detroit. However, despite almost doubling his wage bill, he still increased his profits.

SOURCE 4 The Model T was standardised to the last degree. Ford realised that if cars could be produced more cheaply, more people would be able to buy them; and, as demand rose and the company sold more cars, he could make them even cheaper. The price of the Model T fell continuously throughout the 1920s

The impact of the Model T

Ford more than anyone else started the enormous growth in car ownership. He wanted ordinary Americans to have their own cars.

When the Model T first came out, its price was $1200; by 1928 it was $295. The Model T was a uniquely popular car. Its huge, rear springs made it almost wobble along but allowed it to run on rutted mud roads and gravel tracks. Its rear wheel could be taken off and a power belt run from the hub to a circular saw or farm machine. The Model T got a farmer to town in half an hour and released his wife from the isolation of the farmhouse. It brought an immense sense of freedom to rural America.

Making the car affordable changed the face of America. It encouraged the building of roads and the development of suburbs. It also changed the way people lived their lives (see page 36). The car contributed to the boom of the 1920s by stimulating growth in other industries; for instance, 90 per cent of petrol, 80 per cent of rubber, and 75 per cent of plate glass were consumed by cars in the mid-1920s when one in every two cars was a Model T. Fifteen million had been built by the time production was ended in 1928.

5. Why do you think the Model T was so popular with many Americans in the 1920s?
6. Why was its impact on America so great? Give at least three reasons.
7. Do you agree with the writer of Source 8?

SOURCE 5 Henry Ford

It is better to sell a large number of cars at a reasonable small margin than to sell fewer cars at a larger margin of profit. I hold this because it enables a large number of people to buy and enjoy the use of a car and because it gives a larger number of men employment at good wages.

3. Why was mass-production so important to the development of industry?
4. Why could Ford constantly reduce the price of cars but still make huge profits?

SOURCE 6 A farmer's wife in 1918 wrote to Henry Ford

You know, Henry, your car has lifted us out of the mud. It brought joy to our lives. We loved every rattle in its bones.

SOURCE 7 Alastair Cooke, *America*, 1973

It is staggering to consider what the Model T was to lead to in both industry and folkways. It certainly wove the first network of paved highways ... Beginning in the early 1920s, people who had never taken a holiday beyond the nearest lake or mountain could now explore the South, New England, even the West, and in time the whole horizon of the United States. Most of all, the Model T gave to the farmer and the rancher, miles from anywhere, a new pair of legs.

SOURCE 8 Daniel Snowman, *USA, the Twenties to Vietnam*, 1968

As the first great mass-producer of automobiles, Ford might be said to have done more than any other person to alter out of all recognition the society into which he had been born.

8. What factors do you think made Henry Ford such a successful businessman (see also page 29)?

Henry Ford
Rich man of influence

SOURCE 9 Henry Ford with his son

Henry Ford was a determined man with strong views. He liked to live a simple life, did not drink, and had a strong sense of morality. However, he could treat people harshly if they did not do what he wanted. Because Henry Ford was so rich and famous, Americans took note of what he said on matters other than business. He had the ear of powerful people and tried to influence national policy.

Pacifist

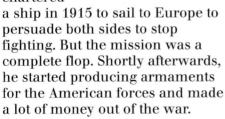

A pacifist opposed to the First World War, Ford chartered a ship in 1915 to sail to Europe to persuade both sides to stop fighting. But the mission was a complete flop. Shortly afterwards, he started producing armaments for the American forces and made a lot of money out of the war.

Politician

Ford stood for election as a senator and was popular with farmers and Prohibitionists. However, he refused to campaign or make speeches, and lost the election. In the early 1920s, a Ford-for-President movement developed but Ford quickly put a stop to it.

Anti-Semite

For most of the 1920s, Ford used his personal newspaper, the *Deerborn Gazette*, to launch vicious attacks on Jews. He blamed an international Jewish conspiracy for starting the war. He claimed that Jewish bankers were trying to take control of American agriculture and were cheating farmers. Ford's articles were circulated widely and encouraged anti-Semitism throughout America. Ford stopped his attacks suddenly in 1927 but the damage to the Jewish community had been done.

Union basher

Ford was violently anti-trade union. He had a network of spies to inform on any workers who had union sympathies. If they did they could be beaten up and sacked from their jobs. The men had no representation in assembly-line work which aged them prematurely and then discarded them. Ford encouraged other employers to resist unions with strong-arm tactics.

Charity giver

Ford built his own hospital, maintained an orphanage and gave millions to schools and colleges. He favoured work-schools which taught trades to boys. One of his most significant contributions to American society was the Henry Ford Museum at Greenfield. In a vast site, he collected objects – tools, steam engines, cars – that he thought would show more about America's real past than dull history books. He even brought whole buildings including Thomas Edison's laboratory and the Wright brothers' bicycle shop. Millions of people still visit the museum every year.

■ TASK

Write an essay on the significance of Henry Ford. Use the ideas below to help you get started. Begin with the points you think were **most** significant about Ford and his role in American history.

- ■ Harmed the Jewish community in America
- ■ Developed mass-production techniques
- ■ Maker of the Model T
- ■ Involvement in politics
- ■ Inventive business ideas
- ■ Built a unique history museum.

Why didn't everyone benefit from the boom?

IN THE 1920s while the rich got richer, the poor made little headway. Many families became poorer during the 1920s. In 1928 the number of people living below the poverty line – those who do not earn enough to buy basic food, clothing and shelter – increased to an estimated 42 per cent of the American population.

Groups who did not share the prosperity of the 1920s

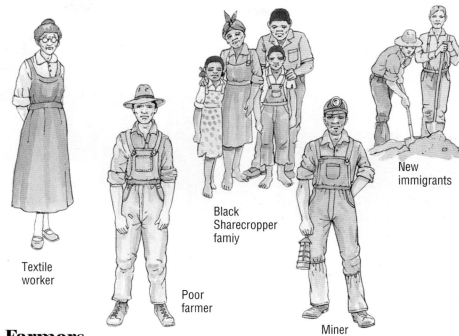

Textile worker

Poor farmer

Black Sharecropper famiy

Miner

New immigrants

SOURCE 1 Farm income

SOURCE 2 A cartoon commenting on the farmers' situation in the 1920s

Farmers

The farming community had a hard time in the 1920s. Some 30 million people earned a living through farming, and half of Americans lived in rural areas, often making their income from selling machinery or providing services to farmers.

New machines, such as the combine-harvesters, made American farming the most efficient in the world, but it was producing far more food than Americans needed. During the war, the surplus had been sold to Europe. After the war European farmers could grow enough to meet their own needs, and the USA faced competition from Canadian farmers who were supplying a vast amount of grain to the world market. The price of grain collapsed and brought ruin to many small farmers. More than three million farming families were earning less than $1000 a year.

As their income dropped, farmers found it difficult to keep up mortgage payments. Some were evicted while others sold their land to clear debts. Between 1920 and 1930 the number of farms declined for the first time in American history. Farm labourers also found themselves out of work, particularly as mechanisation meant that fewer were required. Many went as migrant workers to California. Others went to industrial cities. Those that remained on the land often barely scraped a living.

Not all farmers suffered. Big, mechanised farms did well. The Midwestern grain growers and the California and Florida fruit growers made a good living by shipping their produce in large quantities. It was the small farmers and the labourers who lost out.

1. What were the main problems facing farmers in the 1920s?
2. What point is the cartoonist making in Source 2?
3. In what ways would the poverty of the farmers affect other people who lived in the countryside?

SOURCE 3 Harvesting machinery at work, 1923

4. Source 3 shows a large farming machine. To what extent do you think that the use of such machines was the main cause of farmers' problems? Explain your answer.

Blacks

The biggest concentration of black people was in the southern states of the USA where they were either labourers or SHARECROPPERS (they paid a share of their crops to the landowner). Three-quarters of a million black farm workers lost their jobs during the 1920s. Many blacks made the journey northwards to find work in the cities. By the end of the decade 25 per cent of black people were living in northern cities.

In these cities blacks certainly had greater opportunities than in the South but they still faced discrimination. Sixty per cent of black women in the northern city of Milwaukee worked as low-paid domestic servants in white households. Car factories only hired blacks in small numbers; most operated an all-white policy.

New immigrants

New immigrants who arrived just before or after the war also faced discrimination. They took whatever work they could get, partly because they were often less educated than other workers.

A large number worked in construction where there was a building boom. But construction workers' wages only rose four per cent in the 1920s because the immigrants were a supply of cheap labour and more of the work was becoming mechanised. The unemployment rate amongst new immigrants remained high throughout the decade.

SOURCE 4 A black family living in Harlem, New York, c. 1920

34

People who worked in old industries

Older industries were undergoing modernisation, particularly mechanisation, in the 1920s. Some industries such as steel, for which there was a huge demand, benefited from general expansion. But workers in others, particularly the raw materials industries – cotton, coal, tin and copper – were suffering. There was overproduction (more was produced than could be sold) in these industries, prices dropped and wages fell.

The story of coal was typical. Too much coal was being produced and the market was shrinking as oil, gas and electricity were increasingly used as alternatives. Mines closed and wages were cut. Safety standards dropped, and the working day grew longer. In 1922 600,000 miners went on a four-month strike for better conditions but to no avail. The unions were broken as non-union mines charged less for their coal and got more of the market (65 per cent in 1926).

SOURCE 6 An immigrant family in the living room of a tenement in New York. Housing conditions for many immigrants in the cities were extremely bad. The tenements were damp, dirty and overcrowded

SOURCE 7 Miners walking out of the mine at the start of a four-month coal strike, March 1922

■ TASK

In 1929 President Hoover said, 'We in America today are nearer to the final triumph over poverty than ever before in the history of any land.'

As an opponent of the Republicans, collect evidence from this section (text and sources) to write a report for Hoover explaining why he is wrong. Provide evidence of:

■ how the different groups are suffering
■ the problems in farming, coal and textiles.

SOURCE 5 The cotton and wool industries were faced with competition from new artificial fibres such as rayon. Textile workers were among the lowest paid. In 1926, there was a strike at the Loray cotton mill in North Carolina where male workers were paid $18 per week, women workers $9 per week, compared with an average weekly wage in New York City of $200 per week

HOW WAS SOCIETY CHANGING IN THE 1920s?

Changing attitudes and values

THE PROSPERITY OF the 1920s brought a change in lifestyle for many Americans: more people owned their own homes and cars, and had labour-saving devices to help with housework. They had more leisure time and more money to spend. The entertainment industry grew, with dancehalls and clubs opening up. There were wider changes in social attitudes. People were influenced by what they heard on the radio and saw at the cinema. Prohibition encouraged wild partying where alcohol flowed freely. The fact that it was illegal made it all the more exciting. This was, after all, the 'Roaring Twenties'.

> **SOURCE 1** R. and H. Lynd, *Middletown in Transition*, 1937; car ownership was seen as very important
>
> *We'd rather do without clothes than give up the car. I never feel as close to my family as I do when we are together in the car.*

The car

The impact of the car on life in the USA cannot be exaggerated. It gave people great freedom to travel, whether to visit friends or take day trips to the cities. Many people moved out to live in the suburbs during the 1920s because they could drive into work. The car meant that young people could escape their parents and go off to cinemas or clubs. Not everybody was in favour of the car: some people thought that it was leading to a moral decline in young people, giving them the 'opportunity for sexual freedom'; others blamed it for making crime easier.

Radio

America's first radio station – Station KDKA – was started in 1920. The radio quickly became an important part of life. By 1930 40 per cent of all homes in the USA had a radio set. The radio gave Americans access to new types of music from dance bands to jazz. It also created a national habit – listening to sporting events that they could not go to see. Sporting personalities, like baseball stars, became national figures because of the radio.

SOURCE 2 College students in a Ford car, 1926

SOURCE 3 Babe Ruth, the most famous baseball player in the 1920s

Clubs and dancing

Visiting clubs and dancehalls became enormously popular in the 1920s. The slow, formal dances of pre-war America were replaced by fast dances like the Charleston and more rhythmic dances that had a more openly sexual element to them. Dancing had such a dramatic effect that many people condemned it (see Source 5).

SOURCE 4 Dancing the Charleston in Broadway. Before the war dancing had been formal and slow. It gave way to fast, rhythmic dances like the Charleston

SOURCE 5 Rev. Burke Culpepper, at Mount Vernon Methodist Episcopal Church, 1925

66 *Dancing is a divorce feeder. It is heathen, animalistic and damnable. It degrades womanhood and manhood. Now is the time to say plainly that it is one of the most pernicious of all modern customs.* 99

Jazz

The 1920s has been called the 'Jazz Age'. This is because black music – whether jazz, blues or soul – dominated all other music at this time. It arrived with the great black migration to the northern cities and had a tremendous impact on the young. It fed into dancehalls, popular music and stage musicals. Older people saw it as a corrupting influence linked to sexual excess, as Source 7 shows.

SOURCE 7 Anne Shaw Faulkner, 'Does Jazz Put the Sin in Syncopation?', in *Ladies' Home Journal*, 1921

66 *Jazz originally was the accompaniment of the voodoo dancer, stimulating the half-crazed barbarian to the vilest deeds. The weird chant has been employed by other barbaric people to stimulate brutality and sensuality. That it has a demoralizing effect on the human brain has been demonstrated by many scientists ... Jazz stimulates to extreme deeds, to a breaking away from all rules and conventions; it is harmful and dangerous, and its influence is wholly bad.* 99

SOURCE 6 Duke Ellington, the famous jazz composer, pianist and band leader

37

Sex and the cinema

One of the biggest areas of change and controversy was sexual morals. Sex outside marriage became more common, and contraceptive advice was openly available for the first time. A big gap was developing between the attitudes of young people and their parents.

Young Americans in particular visited the cinema two or three times per week. They were greatly affected by what they saw on screen and by the lives of the 'stars' off screen. People wanted to know what their favourite stars were wearing and doing – and to copy the fads and fashions in their own lives. Studio publicity agents made sure that the magazines got all the information they needed to keep their readers interested.

The much freer sex of the 1920s horrified many older Americans. They blamed the cinema for its blatant use of sex symbols such as Clara Bow and Rudolf Valentino.

They were shocked by the morality in Hollywood films and by the private lives of some of the screen stars. Public scandals, like the mysterious death of a young girl at a party given by Fatty Arbuckle (a famous comic film star), led to a call for censorship. But Hollywood got in first by setting up the Hays code which specified that: 'no film shall be produced which shall lower the moral standards of those who see it. Hence the sympathy of the audience shall never be thrown to the side of crime, wrong-doing, evil or sin.' Nudity was not allowed and the length of kisses was restricted.

SOURCE 8 Clara Bow – the 'It' Girl. Everyone knew that It meant sex

SOURCE 9 An advertisement for the movie *Alimony*, 1925

66 *Brilliant men, beautiful jazz babies, champagne baths, midnight revels, petting parties in the purple dawn, all ending in one terrific smashing climax that makes you gasp.* 99

SOURCE 10 Rudolf Valentino was the first male star to be sold on sex appeal. The studio publicity machine reported how women fainted when they saw him. When Valentino died tragically in 1926 people filled the streets outside the funeral parlour where the body lay, and 100,000 filed past his corpse. A hundred were injured in the struggle to gain admittance

SOURCE 11 Theda Bara (real name Theodosia Goodman) was manufactured to be a 'bad girl' – her film name was an anagram of 'Arab Death'. She was said to have occult powers and be frightfully wicked. Her first picture, *A Fool There Was*, created a sensation. For years the film's most famous line, 'kiss me, my fool', was a popular catch-phrase

1. How do Sources 8–11 show why the cinema was regarded as responsible for the decline in morality?
2. Study the painting in Source 12 carefully.
a) List all the activities you can spot.
b) Look at the woman on the right: note all the points about her that suggest changes in women's lives and their position in society.
c) What impression of the 1920s do you get from the painting?
d) In what ways is this painting useful to historians writing about changing lifestyles in the 1920s?
3. Copy and complete a chart like the one below, using evidence from pages 36–39.

Why some people saw the 1920s as an exciting period of changes in behaviour and attitudes	Why some people saw the 1920s as a very worrying decade of moral decline

SOURCE 12 Mural, *Entertainment*, by Thomas Hart Benton

How was life different for women in the 1920s?

DURING THE 1920s there were many signs that the role of women was changing. The war had brought about two big changes:

- Women had been given the vote in 1920. This gave them more political power.
- Women had worked in wartime factories in large numbers. This proved they could do the jobs just as well as men, and gave many women the desire for more work opportunities.

Work

Increasing numbers of women were entering work, particularly as mechanisation in many manufacturing industries meant that physical strength was not so important. In the radio industry they were the preferred employees. There was also a great expansion in office work with many young women being taken on. One of the reasons why employers were willing to employ women was that they could pay them lower wages than men. By the end of the decade there were over 10 million women in paid employment – a 25 per cent increase on 1920.

Social habits

Some of the social restrictions women had faced before the war had weakened. Clothes had changed: the tight-waisted, ankle-length, voluminous dresses of pre-war days had been replaced by waistless knee-length, lightweight dresses. These gave greater freedom of movement as well as being more daring.

Before the war, women had been expected to have long hair. After the war short hair became a sign of liberation. Make-up became popular and sales boomed, led by advertisements. In the 1920s, women smoked in public and drove cars, both of which would have been frowned upon before the war. Middle-class women had more free time, partly through the new domestic labour-saving products like vacuum cleaners. If they had a car (as many did) they were no longer so bound to the home.

Advertising was aimed specifically at women as the people who took most of the spending decisions in a family. Some historians suggest that Henry Ford abandoned his 'black only' policy for cars because women wanted coloured cars. Women's magazines sold in their millions, and the radio and cinema were well aware that women formed a major part of their audience.

SOURCE 1 A school teacher in 1905

SOURCE 2 Young American women wearing the new style of clothing which became popular after the war

SOURCE 3 Women in Chicago being arrested for wearing banned one-piece bathing suits. The old all-concealing swimsuits gave way to new figure-hugging costumes

FLAPPER was a name given to a liberated urban woman. Few women would have regarded themselves as flappers. But the flapper represented an extreme example of the changes that were affecting many women. They were identified by their short skirts, bobbed hair, powdered knees, bright clothes and lots of make-up.

SOURCE 4 Women from the 1920s:
a) Two flappers on motor cycles;
b) A flapper wearing the latest, sophisticated fashions, 1927

a

b

SOURCE 5 Bruce Bliven, in *New Republic*, 1925, wrote an article called 'Flapper Jane'. Below is an extract

❝ *'Jane,' say I, 'I am a reporter representing American inquisitiveness. Why do you dress the way you do?'...*

'In a way,' says Jane, 'it's just honesty. Women have come down off the pedestal lately. They are tired of this mysterious feminine-charm stuff. Maybe it goes with independence, earning your own living and voting and all that...

Women still want to be loved... but they want it on a 50–50 basis, which includes being admired for the qualities they really possess. Dragging in this strange-allurement stuff doesn't seem sporting...

Of course, not so many girls are looking for a life mealticket nowadays. Lots of them prefer to earn their own living and omit the home-and-baby act. Well, anyhow, postpone it years and years. They think a bachelor girl can and should do everything a bachelor man does.' ❞

1. Use the sources and information here to explain:

 ■ the ways life was changing for women
 ■ whether these changes meant a better life.

2. How does the difference between Sources 1 and 2 show some of these changes?

3. Why is the flapper (Source 4) taken as the symbol of the changes?

4. a) What explanations does Flapper Jane in Source 5 give for these changes?

 b) How useful do you think Source 5 is as evidence of women's opinions?

Does the picture of changing roles for women hold good across the whole of the USA?

SOURCE 6 Doris E. Fleischman, *America As Americans See It*, F.J. Ringel (ed.), 1932

❝ *It is wholly confusing to read the advertisements in the large magazines that feature the enticing qualities of vacuum cleaners, mechanical refrigerators and hundreds of other devices which should lighten the chores of women in the home. On the whole these large middle classes do their own housework with few of the mechanical aids ...*

Among 10,000 farm houses, only 32 per cent have any running water at all; 96 per cent do their own washing. Only 57 per cent use washing machines. A meagre 47 per cent have carpet sweepers.

Women who live on farms – and they form the largest group in the United States – do a great deal of work besides the labour of caring for their children, washing the clothes, caring for the home and cooking ... thousands still labour in the fields ... help milk the cows ...

The other largest group of American women comprise the families of the labourers ... of the miners, the steel workers ... the vast army of unskilled, semi-skilled and skilled workers. The wages of these men are on the whole so small (that) wives must do double duty – that is, caring for the children and the home and toil on the outside as wage earners. ❞

SOURCE 7 For thousands of American women in rural areas, the 1920s did not bring many changes. They continued to play traditional roles

SOURCE 8 J.T. Patterson, *America in the Twentieth Century*

❝ *Though a few upper middle-class women in the cities talked about throwing off the older conventions – they were the flappers – most women stuck to more traditional attitudes concerning 'their place' ... most middle-class women concentrated on managing the home ... Their daughters far from taking to the streets against sexual discrimination were more likely to prepare for careers as mothers and housewives. Millions of immigrant women and their daughters ... also clung to traditions that placed men firmly in control of the family. Most American women concentrated on making ends meet or setting aside money to purchase the new gadgets that offered some release from household drudgery.* ❞

5. Look carefully at Sources 6–11 and the information on Middletown. How far do you think these sources support the impression of women's freedom given on pages 40–41. Do they:

   ■ completely disagree and show a different picture?
   ■ agree in some ways and not in others?
   ■ agree in many ways?

   Use specific examples from the sources to support whichever answer you have chosen.
6. Does the evidence here support the historian's conclusion in Source 8?
7. From Sources 6–11 choose the two which helped you most in finding out about changes in women's lives. Explain why you chose these sources.

Middletown woman

In the early 1920s two researchers led a team of people in a survey of the life of a small American town. In the book they wrote about it they did not name their town but called it Middletown. It was in fact Mucie, Indiana. It gives us one of the most complete portraits of American women and home life in this period that is available.

Summary of some of the findings

86% owned their own homes.
99% of homes wired for electricity. Electricity consumption had gone up by 25% in four years.

Differences between middle-and working-class homes

Middle class	Working class
All homes had a telephone	Half had a telephone
All had a car	60% had a car
None of the housewives got up before 6 a.m.	40% of housewives got up before 5 a.m., 90% before 6 a.m.

SOURCE 9 Items sold by five electrical goods shops in Middletown May–October 1923

66 *Curlers*   *1173*
Irons   *1114*
Vacuum cleaners   *709*
Toasters   *463*
Washing machines   *371*
Heaters   *114*
Fridges   *11* 99

Views of women on women's issues

■ Women should make a good home for their husbands and care for children but also earn money outside the home.
■ Mothers thought that the behaviour of their daughters was changing; for example, they didn't want to learn sewing. They wanted to go out, they were more aware of sex, largely through the cinema, and were more likely to make the first moves on boys.
■ Labour-saving devices had helped ease the burden of housework. Running water, coal fires (instead of wood) and linoleum floors (instead of wood or stone) had helped to reduce domestic chores. Canned goods, bakers' bread, and ready-made clothing were also very helpful.

SOURCE 10 Comments of middle- and working-class mothers on their daughters

66 *Girls aren't so modest nowadays; they dress differently.*

It's the girls' clothing; we can't keep our boys decent when girls dress that way.

Girls have more nerve nowadays – look at their clothes!

Girls are far more aggressive today. They call the boys up to try to make dates with them as they never would when I was a girl. 99

SOURCE 11 The views of Dorothy Dix who wrote the advice column in the local newspaper that was read by the majority of Middletown women

66 *The old idea used to be that the way a woman helps her husband was by being thrifty and industrious, by peeling the potatoes a little thinner and making over her old hats and frocks. But the woman who makes of herself nothing but a domestic drudge is not a help to her husband. She is a hindrance and a man's wife is the show window where he exhibits the measure of his achievement.*

Good looks are a girl's trump card. Dress well and appear 50% better looking than you are, make yourself charming, cultivate bridge and dancing, the ability to play jazz and a few outdoor sports ... In general brains seems to be regarded as of small importance in a wife. 99

chapter 5

HOW WIDESPREAD WAS INTOLERANCE IN THE 1920s?

The Red Scare

AS WE SAW on page 18, attitudes to new immigrants to the USA were changing well before the First World War. Established Americans thought that letting more people in was only adding to America's problems and was diluting America's 'true' Anglo-Saxon (white, European) nature. The idea that the USA should welcome all who wanted to come was losing popularity.

The war increased these feelings, particularly after the BOLSHEVIK REVOLUTION in Russia which brought into being the world's first communist state. Some Americans were worried about being swamped by people from southern and eastern Europe who brought communist and anarchist beliefs with them. They classed people who held these 'un-American' ideas under the general heading 'Reds'.

Strikes

Fears about Reds grew after the war. A wave of strikes in 1919 – 3600 strikes involving 400,000 workers – convinced Americans that communists were trying to destroy their way of life. This was the beginning of the 'Red Scare' which was at its height between 1919 and 1921.

In Seattle in 1919, a general strike seemed to the American public to be evidence of a Red communist plot led by an organisation called the Industrial Workers of the World (IWW), and nicknamed the 'Wobblies'. Later, coal-miners, steel-workers and even the police force of the city of Boston went on strike. As workers in industry after industry went on strike they were locked out, sacked or starved into defeat. Many disputes turned to violence as employers, with government approval, used heavy-handed tactics.

The strikes were largely the result of terrible working conditions and low pay. Workers in heavy industries often worked twelve or more hours a day, and wages between 1914 and 1919 had fallen way behind the cost of living. But neither the public nor the government were interested in the plight of the workers. The authorities reacted to the strikes as though they were the start of a communist revolution to take over America.

Bombs

The fear of radicalism was greatly increased by a series of bombing incidents during 1919, including one which destroyed part of the home of the Attorney-General, Mitchell Palmer. The press whipped up hysteria, and mobs and police attacked socialist parades on May Day. Socialist organisations were raided and their books and pamphlets seized.

SOURCE 1 Newspaper headlines at the time of the bombings in 1919

> **" 36 WERE MARKED AS VICTIMS OF BOMB CONSPIRATORS**
>
> **REDS PLANNED MAY DAY MURDERS**
>
> **BEWARE BOX IF IT COMES THROUGH MAIL – DO NOT OPEN IT – CALL THE POLICE BOMB SQUAD**
>
> **RED PERIL HERE "**

The Palmer Raids

After the attack on his home, Mitchell Palmer devoted himself to rounding up anyone he believed was a 'Red'. During the 'Palmer Raids', between 4000 and 6000 suspected communists were arrested in 36 cities across the USA. In the end, 556 'aliens' were deported, but it was shown that most of those arrested were not communist supporters.

Despite the fiasco of the Palmer Raids, the alarms and hysteria of the 'Red Scare' continued throughout the 1920s. Some people used it as an excuse to attack any groups that they disliked or distrusted – Catholics, Jews, blacks, or new immigrants. Trade unionists were regarded as 'un-American' and unions were considerably weakened in the 1920s by raids and persecution.

SOURCE 3 Billy Sunday, an evangelist and popular hero, quoted in the *Seattle Post-Intelligencer*, 3 May 1919. He is describing a Bolshevik

66 *... a guy with a face like a porcupine and breath that would scare a pole cat. If I had my way, I'd fill the jails so full with them that their feet would stick out the windows ... Let them rule – we'll swim our horses in blood up to the bridles first.* 99

SOURCE 2 A cartoon entitled 'Come On!', which appeared in the San Francisco *Examiner* in September 1919. The American Legion was formed in 1919 to uphold traditional American values and the Constitution, and maintain law and order. It was a patriotic organisation with men full of 'pep, punch and democracy'

SOURCE 4 Socialist newspapers claimed that the bombings were the work of right-wing extremists to encourage the government and others to attack the socialists. The *Liberator* (socialist newspaper) said

66 *We believe that the reason that the perpetrators of these extensive and elaborate dynamitings have not been discovered is that some important person does not want to discover them.* 99

SOURCE 5 Next door to Palmer's house was found an anarchist pamphlet, the *Plain Truth*

66 *There will have to be bloodshed; we will not dodge; there will have to be murder; we will kill ... there will have to be destruction; we will destroy ... We are ready to do anything to suppress the capitalist system.* 99

1. Why were 'established' Americans suspicious of the new immigrants?
2. Why did Americans believe that 'Reds' were active in America?
3. Look at Source 2.
a) Who do the people in the cartoon represent?
b) What do you think the words on the baseball bat mean?
c) What is the cartoonist's message?
d) Do you think the cartoonist is a socialist?
4. What effect do you think Billy Sunday's words (Source 3) and the headlines in Source 1 would have had on Americans?
5. a) What, according to Source 4, is the socialist version of the bombings?
b) How reliable is the *Liberator* as a source about events at this time?
6. In view of Source 5, do you think the American public was right to be scared?
7. What were the consequences of the Red Scare?

How and why did American immigration policy change in the 1920s?

MANY OF THE newer immigrants moved into ghettos in the big cities (see page 18). These were often harsh places. Americans felt threatened by different nationalities who spoke their own language rather than English. Americans blamed the new immigrants for the rising violence and problems in the cities.

In 1921 the Republicans won the election and Warren Harding became President – that year immigration was limited to 357,000 people.

1921 Immigration Quota Act

A quota system was introduced: new immigrants were allowed in in proportion to the number of people of the same nationality who had been in America in 1910. The figure was set at 3 per cent.

1924 National Origins Act

The quota was reduced to 2 per cent of the 1890 census. Since there had been more people from northern Europe, e.g. English and Irish, in America in 1890, more of these groups were allowed to enter.

1929

Only 150,000 immigrants per year were allowed in. There were to be no Asians at all. Northern and western Europeans were to be allocated 85 per cent of all places.

The intention of the nationality-based quotas was to restrict the number of people from southern and eastern Europe, Japan and China. By 1930, immigration to the USA from these areas had virtually stopped.

SOURCE 1 In the election campaign of 1920 the Republican Party described their immigration policy in this way

66 *The immigration policy of the U.S. should be such as to insure that the number of foreigners in the country at any one time shall not exceed that which can be assimilated with reasonable speed, and to favour immigrants whose standards are similar to ours.* 99

SOURCE 2 In 1921, a Senator from Alabama gave this explanation of why he wanted more immigration controls

66 *The steamship companies haul them over to America, and as soon as they step off the decks of their ships the problem of the steamship companies is settled, but our problem has begun – bolshevism, red anarchy, black-handers and kidnappers, challenging the authority and integrity of our flag ...*

Thousands come here who never take the oath to support our Constitution and to become citizens of the United States. They pay allegiance to some other country while they live upon the substance of our own. They fill places that belong to the loyal wage-earning citizens of America ... They are of no service whatever to our people. They constitute a menace and a danger to us every day ... 99

1. What do you think the Republican Party hoped to achieve by their immigration policy?
2. What do Sources 1 and 2 suggest were the main reasons behind this policy?
3. How do these laws go against the original spirit of America as summed up by the Statue of Liberty (see page 8)?

Why were Sacco and Vanzetti executed?

ON 15 APRIL 1920 Fred Parmenter, the paymaster of a shoe factory in South Braintree, and an armed guard were attacked by two men who opened fire on them. The attackers escaped with $15,000. Before he died Parmenter was able to say that his attackers had been slim foreigners with olive skins. The guard also died soon afterwards.

On 5 May 1920 two Italian-born labourers – Nicola Sacco and Bartolomeo Vanzetti – were arrested and charged with the murder of Parmenter and the guard. Both Sacco and Vanzetti were self-confessed ANARCHISTS and hated capitalism and the American system of government. Sacco and Vanzetti were tried before Judge Webster Thayer. Their trial began in May 1921 and lasted 45 days.

The trial took place at the height of the Red Scare. It aroused such strong emotions among the American people that it took a week to find a jury of twelve men (out of the 875 who were called to the court) that were acceptable to both the defence and the prosecution. The jury in the trial retired to consider their verdict on 14 July 1921. They returned a verdict of guilty the same day. Sacco and Vanzetti were sentenced to death.

The trial was unusual in that it was reported in newspapers all over the world. There were demonstrations in cities across the world in support of Sacco and Vanzetti. The American Embassy in Paris was bombed as a protest against the verdict. The protesters claimed that the trial had not been fairly conducted, and that Sacco and Vanzetti were being singled out because of their politics and their race.

SOURCE 1 Sacco and Vanzetti

SOURCE 2 A protest in London against the execution of Sacco and Vanzetti, 1927

Their case was taken to appeal in higher courts, but none of them would overturn the original verdict. The process dragged on for six years. The last unsuccessful appeal was heard in 1927. Sacco and Vanzetti were put to death in the electric chair on 24 August 1927.

In the 1970s the Governor of Massachusetts granted Sacco and Vanzetti a formal pardon and accepted that a mistrial had taken place.

The trial

Below is a summary of the evidence which the prosecution and defence brought to the trial of Sacco and Vanzetti.

Evidence for the prosecution

- 61 eyewitnesses identified them as the killers. They were sure some Italian-looking men did it.
- Sacco and Vanzetti were both carrying loaded guns at the time of their arrests.
- Forensic experts say that Sacco's pistol matched the pistol that killed the guard.
- The prosecution said Sacco and Vanzetti had acted in a guilty manner when they were arrested and had lied to the police.
- Vanzetti had a previous conviction for armed robbery in December 1919.

Evidence for the defence

- 107 people confirmed Sacco and Vanzetti's alibi that they were somewhere else at the time of the crime. But most of them were recent Italian immigrants who could hardly speak any English.
- The prosecution witnesses did not agree on details, e.g. what the men were wearing at the time of the crime, and many changed their evidence by the time of the trial.
- A number of other men confessed to being the murderers.
- It was not a crime to carry a gun (many Americans did). Sacco and Vanzetti were worried about being attacked because of their political beliefs.
- The ballistic evidence on the guns was very dubious – there were rumours it had been rigged.
- Sacco and Vanzetti said that they had lied to the police because they thought they would be victimised because they were foreigners and had radical political beliefs.

SOURCE 3 Sacco and Vanzetti at their trial

SOURCE 4 After the trial Judge Thayer is reported to have said

66 Did you see what I did to those anarchistic bastards the other day? 99

He is also supposed to have called Sacco and Vanzetti 'dagos' and 'sons of bitches' in private conversation during the trial.

SOURCE 5 A leading American lawyer made the following remarks about Judge Thayer

66 I have known Judge Thayer all my life ... I say that he is a narrow-minded man; he is an unintelligent man; he is full of prejudice; he is carried away by fear of Reds, which [has] captured about ninety per cent of the American people. 99

1. What was unusual about Sacco and Vanzetti's trial? (See page 47.)
2. What were the main differences between the evidence for the prosecution and the evidence for the defence? You can use a chart to present your findings.
3. Look at Sources 4 and 5. What do they suggest about Judge Thayer? Do you think he could have been trusted to judge Sacco and Vanzetti fairly?
4. What is the message in the cartoon in Source 6? Is this useful historical evidence about the case?

SOURCE 6 A German cartoon suggesting that Sacco and Vanzetti were praying for the electric chair to save them from the American legal system

SOURCE 7 As they were led from the court, Vanzetti commented

❝ *What I say is that I am innocent . . . It is seven years that we are in jail. What we have suffered no human tongue can say, and yet you see me before you, not trembling, you see me looking in your eyes straight . . . not ashamed or in fear . . . We were tried in a time that has now passed into history. I mean by that, a time when there was hysteria of resentment and hate against the people of our principles, against the foreigner . . .*

I am suffering because I am a radical and indeed I am a radical; I have suffered because I was Italian and indeed I am an Italian; . . . but I am so convinced to be right that if you could execute me two times, and if I could be reborn two other times, I would live again to do what I have done already.

[As he was being led to the electric chair Vanzetti said]

I want to tell you that I am innocent and that I have never committed any crime but sometimes some sin . . . I wish to forgive some people for what they are now doing to me. ❞

SOURCE 8 Robert K. Murray, *Red Scare*, 1955

❝ *Their many sympathisers . . . continued to claim that the word 'anarchist' rather than any criminal act had sent them to the electric chair, and the whole incident was denounced as a prime example of American disdain for justice and prejudice against the foreigner.* ❞

5. Do the statements by Vanzetti in Source 7 prove anything at all?
6. Do you think they were executed because:
a) they were clearly guilty
b) there was a good chance that they were guilty
c) they were Italian-looking
d) they were foreigners and anarchists who were causing trouble
e) undesirable trouble-makers might as well pay for the crime to teach these people a lesson?
Choose one or a combination of the statements above and justify your conclusion.
7. Do you agree/disagree with the opinion expressed in Source 8? Explain your answer.

■ **TASK**

Write a present-day newspaper report on the anniversary of the execution of Sacco and Vanzetti. Look back at the trial and the circumstances in which it took place. Consider the evidence for and against. Draw your own conclusions about why they were executed and whether they would have been executed today.

The rise and fall of the Ku Klux Klan

THE KU KLUX KLAN started in the southern states at the end of the American Civil War in 1864–65. Its aim was to terrorise black people, newly freed from slavery. In 1915 it was revived. This revival was helped by a film called *The Birth of the Nation*, produced by D.W. Griffith. The film was set in the South after the American Civil War and portrayed the Klan saving white families from gangs of blacks intent on looting and rape. The film attracted huge audiences and increased the Klan's popularity. By 1920 the Klan had over 100,000 members; by 1925 it claimed a membership of around five million.

The Klan attracted FANATICS who believed that the best American citizens were white Anglo-Saxon Protestants (WASPs). They were fighting for 'native, white, Protestant supremacy'. They were anti-communist, anti-negro, anti-Jew, anti-Catholic and against **all** foreigners. They believed they were on a moral crusade to protect decent American values.

In the South the Klan focused more specifically on black people, seeking to terrorise them and frighten them into submission. The Klan represented the prejudices and fears of many Americans, especially those who lived in small towns. It had some powerful members, for instance, the Governor of Alabama and a Senator from Texas were Klan members.

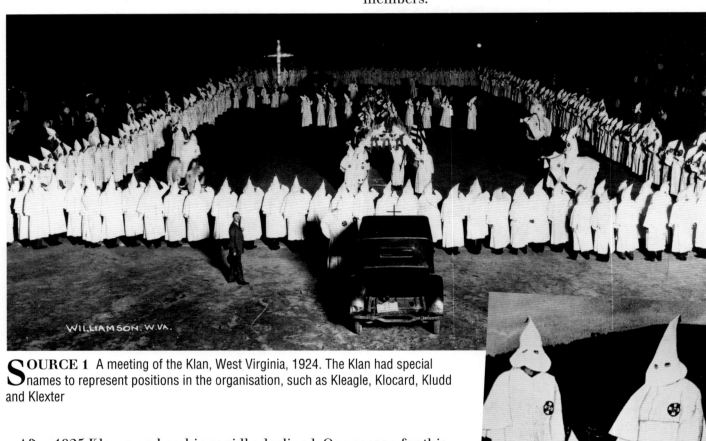

WILLIAMSON, W.VA.

SOURCE 1 A meeting of the Klan, West Virginia, 1924. The Klan had special names to represent positions in the organisation, such as Kleagle, Klocard, Kludd and Klexter

After 1925 Klan membership rapidly declined. One reason for this decline was the excesses of some of its leaders. The 'Imperial Wizard' led the Klan, and each state was under the command of a 'Grand Dragon'. The Grand Dragon in Indiana, D.C. Stephenson, was put on trial for raping and mutilating a female assistant, Madge Oberholzer. Reports said that she was covered in vicious bite marks made by human teeth. The case attracted a great deal of publicity, especially as the victim took an overdose after the attack and gave her evidence against Stephenson in a sworn statement from her death bed. Stephenson was found guilty and sentenced to life imprisonment.

SOURCE 2 Ku Klux Klan family group, Georgia 1930

1. What do Sources 1 and 2 tell you about the Klan?

■ SOURCE INVESTIGATION

What were the aims and beliefs of the Ku Klux Klan?

SOURCE 3 From the ten questions that were put to all would-be Klansmen before they were allowed to join

66 2 Are you a native-born, Gentile, American citizen?

3 Are you absolutely opposed to . . . any cause, government, people, sect or ruler that is foreign to the USA?

4 Do you believe in the tenets of the Christian religion?

5 Do you esteem the USA and its institutions above any other government . . . in the whole world?

8 Do you believe in and will faithfully strive for the eternal maintenance of white supremacy? 99

SOURCE 4 In 1926, in a Kansas newspaper, the Klan described who they were fighting against

66 . . . every criminal, every gambler, every thug, every libertine, every girl-ruiner, every home-wrecker, every wife-beater, every dope-peddler, every moonshiner, every crooked politician, every pagan papist priest . . . every Roman controlled newspaper, every hyphenated American, every lawless alien . . . 99

SOURCE 5 R. Coughlan, 'Konclave in Kokomo', in *The Aspirin Age 1919–49*

66 It may be asked why, then, did the town take so enthusiastically to the Klan? . . . Many old stock Americans believed they were in danger of being overrun. The 'foreigners were ruining the country'; and so anything 'foreign' was 'un-American' and a menace. Another important idea in American history was anti-Catholicism because many of the founding fathers had come to America to escape Catholic persecutions in Europe . . .

[Later, Coughlan described a Klan parade]

The road was a creeping mass of cars. They were draped with flags and some carried home-made signs with Klan Slogans as 'America for the Americans' or 'the Pope will sit in the White House when Hell freezes over' . . . That night there was a parade down Main Street in Kokomo. There were thirty bands. They rolled the slow, heavy tempo of the march to a low meadow where the Klan had put up a twenty-five-foot 'fiery cross'. Many of the marchers carried flaming torches. Flag bearers usually carried two Klan flags flanking an American flag, and the word would ripple down the rows of spectators lining the kerbs, 'Here comes the flag!' and 'Hats off for the flag!' 99

SOURCE 6 Klan poem of the 1920s

66 I would rather be a Klansman in a robe of snowy white,
Than to be a Catholic Priest in a robe as black as night,
For a Klansman is an American and America is his home,
But the Priest owes his allegiance to a Dago Pope in Rome. 99

SOURCE 7 William J. Simmons, who helped to make the Klan popular again in 1915

66 America is a garbage can! . . . When the hordes of aliens walk to the ballot box and their votes outnumber yours, then that alien horde has got you by the throat. 99

1. Using Sources 3–7, work out:
a) what the Klan believed in (and who they were against)
b) why so many people supported them in the early 1920s.
2. Why do you think the Klan is so closely associated with patriotism and the American flag (Sources 3 and 5)?
3. What sort of people might have joined the Klan?

SOURCE 8 Abram Smith and Thomas Shipp had been accused of murdering a white man. They were dragged from the jail in the town of Marion in Indiana and were lynched by the mob

SOURCE 9 This is how the *Washington Eagle* described the death of a black man accused of murdering a white woman in Georgia in 1921

  ❝ *The Negro was taken to a grove, where each one of more than 500 people, in Ku Klux Klan ceremonial, had placed a pine knot around a stump, making a pyramid to the height of ten feet. The negro was chained to the stump, and asked if he had anything to say. Castrated and in indescribable torture, the negro asked for a cigarette, lit it and blew the smoke in the face of his tormentors.*

  The pyre was lit and a hundred men and women, old and young, grandmothers among them, joined hands and danced around while the Negro burned. A big dance was held in a barn nearby that evening in celebration of the burning, many people coming by automobile from nearby cities to the gala event. ❞

SOURCE 10 José Yglesias, union activist, describing a strike in 1931 in an interview conducted some years later

  ❝ *During the strike, the KKK would come into the Labor Temple with guns and break up the meetings. Very frequently, they were police in hoods … The picket lines would hold hands, and the KKK would beat them up and cart them off.* ❞

SOURCE 11 R. Coughlan, 'Konclave in Kokomo', in *The Aspirin Age 1919–49*

  ❝ *Once organised in strength, the Klan had an effective weapon in the economic boycott. The anti-Klan merchant saw his trade fade away to the Klan store across the street, where the store window carried a 'TWK' (Trade With Klansmen) sign.* ❞

4. According to Sources 8–11 , what methods did the Klan use to intimidate their enemies?

The black experience in the 1920s

SLAVERY HAD BEEN ended after the American Civil War but blacks continued to suffer discrimination and ill-treatment by whites. Many states passed laws (well into the twentieth century) for the SEGREGATION of blacks in schools, parks, hospitals, swimming pools, libraries and other public places, even cemeteries. These were called 'Jim Crow' laws after a song of 1830, which had presented blacks as childlike and inferior.

Black people found it hard to get fair treatment and were intimidated by whites who tried to control them through fear and terror as shown in Sources 1 and 2 and the pages opposite. The situation was particularly bad in the southern states where most black people lived, often in chronic poverty. Thousands of blacks from 1910 up to the end of the 1920s moved to the cities of the north, hoping to find a better life. For instance, the black population of New York doubled from 150,000 to 300,000 in this period.

But life in the cities was not without its problems. Many blacks found themselves trapped in poverty and living in squalid tenement ghettos. In Chicago, when they tried to use public facilities in the Irish or Polish districts, they were set upon by white gangs calling themselves 'athletic clubs'. One of the most violent years in black American history was 1919, with thousands being driven from their homes in 23 race riots.

The Black Renaissance

However, poverty and discrimination were not the whole story. Black culture and black pride flourished in the cities. Harlem in New York became the centre of an artistic 'RENAISSANCE'. Talented black artists and writers collected there, led by the poet and writer Weldon Johnson. Their work expressed the social and economic grievances of blacks and made whites aware of the 'black experience' of rootlessness and alienation.

Black theatre attracted big audiences and black performing artists – comedians, singers and dancers like Josephine Baker – were successful in musical shows, clubs and black REVUES. Black American music, whether jazz, blues or soul, became one of the most influential art forms of the twentieth century.

1. Explain what the Jim Crow laws were.
2. What evidence is there of unfair treatment for blacks in the South in Sources 1 and 2?
3. Did blacks get a fairer deal in the cities?

SOURCE 1 H.L. Mencken, *Americana*, 1925

❝ Because a juryman failed to agree a verdict of guilty in the case of Alvin Calhoun, a Negro accused of murder, a mob took the juror from the jury-room, whipped him, and dipped him in a mud-hole. After his chastisement he returned to the jury-room and agreed to a verdict of murder in the first degree. ❞

SOURCE 2 From *Miami Herald*, 1925

❝ A small monument made a mysterious appearance . . . yesterday morning. An inscription on one side of the monument reads: 'On this spot a few years ago a white man was found who had been tarred and feathered because he had preached social equality to Negroes.' On another side were the words: 'If you are a reckless Negro or a White man who believes in social equality, be advised Dade county don't need you.' ❞

SOURCE 3 Richard Wright, author of *Native Son*, a moving novel attacking white racism. It set new standards for black literature

SOURCE 4 Langston Hughes

*66 Because my mouth is wide with laughter
And my throat is deep with song
You do not think I suffer
After I have held my pain so long*

*Because my mouth is wide with laughter
You do not hear my inner cry
Because my feet are gay with dancing
You do not know I die? 99*

4. Explain what the 'Black Renaissance' was.
5. What do Sources 4 and 5 tell us about the 'black experience' in American society?

SOURCE 5 Richard Wright, from his autobiography, *Black Boy*. Wright grew up in the 1920s

66 Hunger had always been more or less at my elbow when I played, but now I began to wake up at night to find hunger standing at my bedside. The hunger I had known before this ... had been a normal hunger that had made me beg constantly for bread, and when I ate a crust or two I was satisfied. But this new hunger baffled me, scared me. Whenever I begged for food now my mother would pour me a cup of tea which would still the clamour in my stomach for a moment or two; but a little later I would feel hunger nudging my ribs, twisting my guts until they ached. 99

Political movements

There were major black political movements in the 1920s, the most important of which were the National Association for the Advancement of Coloured People (NAACP) and the Universal Negro Improvement and Conservation Association (UNIA).

NAACP

Led by W.E.B. DuBois, the NAACP was dedicated to 'equal rights and opportunities for all'. It grew rapidly in strength and support, with nearly 90,000 members in some 300 branches in 1919. It was determined to challenge WHITE SUPREMACY, end the segregation laws and make blacks aware of their civil rights, including the right to vote. DuBois was also the father of the PAN-AFRICAN movement in America, recognising the cultural links between black people in Africa and the USA.

One of the NAACP's major campaigns was against the practice of lynching in the South. It carried out investigations which revealed the extent of lynching and proved that it was unjustified and sadistic. It failed to get a law against lynching passed (it was blocked by southern Democrats) but caused public outcry and the number of lynchings fell dramatically.

UNIA

Founded by Marcus Garvey, UNIA was the forerunner of black organisations advocating black power. It reached its peak in 1921 with over a million members.

Garvey said that blacks should have pride in their colour, their culture and their history. He blamed their problems on white racism and he offered disillusioned blacks hope of a better future.

Garvey wanted to establish close contacts with Africa and called on American blacks to use their skills, education and knowledge to make Africa strong and powerful in the world. Garvey pioneered a REPATRIATION 'back to Africa' movement where he encouraged blacks to return to their original homeland to help develop it and escape white racism. UNIA set up the Black Star steamship line to carry migrants and pressed the League of Nations to hand over former colonies to a new African republic, of which Garvey would be president.

Black political movements gained momentum in the 1920s. Newspapers like the *Baltimore Afro-American* and magazines like the *Messenger* helped to spread their views. These movements, especially UNIA, encouraged blacks to set up their own businesses and restaurants, and boycott large stores which would not employ black staff. This had some success and a black middle class, business and professional, began to emerge.

However, Garvey and DuBois fell out badly. Garvey criticised the middle-class blacks of the NAACP for being ashamed of their ancestry and trying to integrate into white society. They, in turn, criticised him for concentrating solely on race and calling for separatism; they also claimed that Garvey's steamship line was cheating its customers. There was some violence between the two movements and in 1923 Garvey was arrested on fraud charges, and later deported to Jamaica. However, the principle of black protest had been established although it took many years for laws to be changed.

6. What were the main differences between the NAACP and UNIA?
7. How successful were black organisations in achieving their aims?

How were native American Indians treated in the 1920s?

In 1924 a law declared that all Indians born in the USA were full citizens of America. However, during the 1920s the white authorities tried to destroy the Indian culture and traditional way of life. Indian children were forced to go to boarding schools, and children from the same tribe were kept apart to destroy any sense of tribal identity. Children found speaking their own language were beaten. At these schools Indian children were encouraged to make fun of their parents and their values. Whole tribes were forced to convert to Christianity and many Indian traditions were banned; for example, performing the Sun Dance, boys having long hair, and the wearing of traditional clothes.

■ **TASK**

Either
Copy and complete the chart below:

In what ways was the 1920s a time of change for black Americans	In what ways did life remain the same for black Americans in the 1920s

Or
As an NAACP member, write an article for the *Baltimore Afro-American* about changes for black Americans in the 1920s.
Mention:

■ what the black community has achieved
■ the success of black culture (writers, musicians etc.)
■ what problems still exist and what needs to be done about these in the future.

Write a short letter from a member of UNIA saying how far you agree/disagree with the article, in particular, how black Americans should act in the future.

SOURCE 4 An Indian logger and his family outside their home on the Tulalip Reservation in Washington

8. Do you think native American Indians were better or worse off than black Americans?

■ **ACTIVITY**

Working in pairs or groups, prepare a radio script for a programme on intolerance in the USA in the 1920s. Select carefully the items you want to use. Consider what you have found out about: immigration, attitudes to foreigners, workers' rights, the Ku Klux Klan, the position of black people and Native American Indians.

What was the Monkey Trial all about?

IN THE 1920s there seemed to be a growing division between urban and rural America. People living in the country were worried about the changes in social attitudes taking place around them, such as the emphasis on material goods, freer sex, provocative dancing and SELF-INDULGENCE. They felt that the easy morals of the cities were tempting their children away from the traditional values of hard work, saving money and clean living.

In the states of the South and Midwest, often called the 'Bible Belt', where church attendance remained high, Christian FUNDAMENTALISTS (who believed that everything in the Bible was literally true) tried to hold 'city vices' at bay. For example, laws were passed which banned the wearing of 'indecent' bathing costumes, petting, the giving of contraceptive advice and gambling on Sunday.

Six states, including Tennessee, also banned the teaching of Charles Darwin's theory of evolution because it contradicted the Bible. According to the Book of Genesis, God had created the world and the universe in six days, whereas Darwin argued that life on earth had evolved gradually over millions of years. This meant humans, monkeys and apes had common ancestors.

To challenge this anti-evolution law in Tennessee, a science teacher called John Scopes agreed to be tried in court for teaching the theory of evolution to his classes. His trial took place in July 1925 in a packed courtroom, with over a hundred newsmen. It was the first trial in American history to be broadcast on the radio. Scopes was defended by America's most famous criminal lawyer, Clarence Darrow. The prosecution was led by fundamentalist, William Jennings Bryan.

There was no real doubt that Scopes had broken the anti-evolution laws and he was fined $100 as a result. However, the trial concentrated on the arguments for and against the theory of evolution. For this reason it became known as the Monkey Trial. Although Scopes was found guilty, the outcome of the trial was generally regarded as a victory for Darrow and the MODERNISTS, and a blow to the fundamentalists who were trying to censor what was taught in schools.

1. Imagine that you are a Christian fundamentalist, living in Tennessee in 1925. Write a letter to the school where your children are taught, explaining why the teaching of Darwin's theory of evolution should be banned and why you have the right to demand this in your children's school.
2. How is Darwin portrayed in Source 1? Why do you think the artist drew him in this way?

SOURCE 1 Cartoon of Darwin in *The Hornet*, 1871

SOURCE 2 Austin Peay, Governor of Tennessee, *Nashville Banner*, 24 March 1925

66 *The people have the right ... to regulate what is taught in their schools. Right or wrong, there is a deep, widespread belief that something is shaking the fundamentals of the country, both in religion and morals. It is the opinion of many that an abandonment of the old-fashioned faith and belief in the Bible is our trouble in a large degree. It is my own belief that the [anti-evolution] law is a popular protest against an irreligious tendency to exalt so-called science, and deny the Bible in some schools.* 99

SOURCE 3 Billy Sunday, a popular evangelist, attacks the teaching of the theory of evolution in schools, 1925

66 *If anyone wants to teach that God-forsaken, hell-born, bastard theory of evolution, then let him ... but do not expect the Christian people of this country to pay for the teaching of a rotten, stinking professor who gets up there and teaches our children to forsake God and makes our schools a clearing-house for their God-forsaken dirty politics.* 99

SOURCE 4 John Scopes surrounded by his legal staff, July 1925

SOURCE 5 Advertisement by American Civil Liberties Union, *Daily Times*, 4 May 1925. The ACLU was set up to fight for freedom of speech and minority rights. It wanted the public to know about its views on the anti-evolution law and other issues. John Scopes replied to the advertisement

66 *We are looking for a Tennessee teacher who is willing to accept our services in testing this law in the courts.* 99

SOURCE 6 J.F. Noris, *World Christian Fundamentalist Association*, 1925. The WCFA aimed to restore traditional religious values. Noris urged William Jennings Bryan to become involved in the case to help spread WCFA views

66 *It is the greatest opportunity ever presented to educate the public and will accomplish more than ten years' campaigning.* 99

SOURCE 7 E. Larson, *Trial and Error*, 1985

66 *Both sides went to Dayton seeking ... to influence popular opinion. Their arguments addressed the world, not the jury. The world listened. Hundreds of reporters descended on Dayton from across America and Europe. Pioneering, live-radio broadcasts carried the event to a fascinated public. Millions followed the progress of the eight-day trial, which was billed as a battle between science and religion.* 99

SOURCE 8 H.L. Mencken, *Baltimore Evening Sun*, July 1925

66 *...for nearly two hours ... Mr Darrow goaded his opponent. [He] asked Mr Bryan if he really believed that the serpent had always crawled on its belly because it tempted Eve, and if he believed Eve was made from Adam's rib ...*

[Bryan's] face flushed under Mr Darrow's searching words, and ... when one stumped him he took refuge in his faith and either refused to answer directly or said in effect: 'The Bible states it; it must be so.' 99

SOURCE 9 Examples of questions Darrow asked Bryan at the trial

66 *Darrow: 'Do you believe in Jonah and the whale?'*
Bryan: 'It is easy to believe in the miracle of Jonah.'
Darrow: 'Do you believe that Joshua made the sun stand still?'
Bryan: 'I believe what the Bible says.'
Darrow: 'Did Eve really come from Adam's rib?'
Bryan: 'Yes.' 99

■ DISCUSSION

Should parents have the right to decide what is taught to their children in schools? Was John Scopes right to break the law?

3. Use Sources 5–7 to explain what the Monkey Trial was really all about. The following questions may help:
a) How did John Scopes come to be the main person in the trial?
b) Why did the ACLU want to get involved in a trial?
c) Why did the WCFA want to get involved in a trial?
d) How was the trial seen from outside Dayton?
4. How did Darrow make a fool of Bryan (Sources 8 and 9)?
5. What was the outcome of the trial?

Prohibition – a noble experiment or a national disaster?

BETWEEN JANUARY 1920 and December 1933 it was against the law to make, sell or transport alcoholic drinks in the USA. This was called 'Prohibition' and it was written into the American Constitution by the 18th Amendment.

Many historians nowadays regard Prohibition as a disastrous mistake which created as many problems in the USA as it solved. Others suggest that while Prohibition may have failed, it was at least a noble experiment. In this section you can decide what you think.

Why did America introduce Prohibition?

Stage 1: the growth of the Temperance movement

The story of Prohibition goes back 100 years to the early 1800s. Temperance (not drinking alcohol) was a common feature of the religious groups who had settled in America in the nineteenth century. But the 'DRIES' (as supporters of Prohibition were called) became stronger with the formation of the Women's Christian Temperance Union in 1873 and the powerful Anti-Saloon League in 1893.

They were particularly strong in the mainly rural areas of the South and the Midwest. They campaigned in each of the states for alcohol to be prohibited within the state. Sources 1–7 show some of the arguments they used. They had such success that by 1914 some states had already banned the making of alcohol.

SOURCE 1 An illustration from a Temperance publication, c. 1820

SOURCE 3 From the *National Temperance Almanac*, 1876

66 *'King Alcohol' has caused more than three-fourths of the pauperism, three-fourths of the crime, and more than one-half of the insanity in the community, and thereby filled our prisons, our alms-houses, and erected the gibbet before our eyes.* 99

SOURCE 4 A song to be sung on marches by 'dry' supporters

66 *I stand for prohibition,*
The utter demolition
Of all this curse of misery and woe;
Complete extermination,
Entire annihilation,
The Saloon must go. 99

SOURCE 5 From a school textbook written by a Prohibitionist

66 *A cat or dog may be killed by causing it to drink a small quantity of alcohol. A boy once drunk whisky from a flask he had found, and died in a few hours.* 99

SOURCE 2 From a sermon by evangelist Billy Sunday

66 *I tell you that the curse of God Almighty is on the saloon.* 99

SOURCE 6 Written by Edwin Theiss, a factory owner

66 *Until booze is banished we can never have really efficient workmen. We are not much interested in the moral side of the matter as such. It is purely a question of dollars and cents.* 99

SOURCE 7 A leaflet published by the Anti-Saloon League in 1919. Between 1909 and 1923 the League printed over one hundred million such leaflets

SOURCE 9 Written by Maud Radford Warren in *Everybody's Magazine*, November 1917

❝ *Every man who works on the land to produce drink instead of bread is a loss in winning the war, and worse, he may mean a dead soldier.* ❞

SOURCE 10 From an Anti-Saloon League pamphlet,1918

❝ *[The American's patriotic duty] is to abolish the un-American, pro-German, crime-producing, food-wasting, youth-corrupting, home-wrecking, treasonable liquor traffic.* ❞

SOURCE 11 Written by the British author G.K. Chesterton in *What I Saw in America*, published in 1922

❝ *Prohibition has been passed in a sort of fever of self-sacrifice, which was a part of the passionate patriotism of America in the war.* ❞

Stage 2: The First World War

By 1917 the Anti-Saloon League had managed to make Prohibition one of the big issues of American politics. At election times every politician was asked where he stood on this issue. Anybody who admitted to 'WET' sympathies knew he would lose hundreds of votes.

When America entered the First World War in 1917 the 'dries' received an enormous boost. It also gave their anti-drink propaganda a boost. The big American brewers were of German descent and had German names. The 'dries' used this to their advantage and portrayed drink as the cause of German aggression. They suggested that refusing alcohol was a patriotic duty.

SOURCE 8 From a speech at the Anti-Saloon League Conference, 1918

❝ *Their sodden habits of life have driven [the Germans] constantly towards brutality and cruelty until they were prepared to strike for universal conquest. Beer will do for a nation what it will for an individual – We need a saloonless and drunkless world.* ❞

1. Which of Sources 1–7 try to frighten people into supporting Prohibition?
2. Which of the country's problems do the 'dries' claim Prohibition will solve?
3. Why might
   a) a church congregation
   b) a factory owner
   have given money to the Anti-Saloon League?
4. How might the Anti-Saloon League have used the money?
5. How did the 'dries' use the First World War to persuade Americans and Congress that Prohibition should be introduced. Refer to Sources 8–11 in your answer.

Why didn't Prohibition work?

NATIONAL PROHIBITION CAME into force on 16 January 1920. It was now against the law to make, sell or transport alcoholic drinks in the USA.

Drinking became secretive and more expensive but it did not stop (consumption was not against the law). The rich had their supplies delivered to their homes. Others might visit a 'speakeasy' – a basement bar behind locked doors with peepholes. The '21 Club' was the speakeasy in New York for the members of high society. There were soon more speakeasies than pre-1919 saloons. By 1925 there were more than 15,000 in the city of Detroit; by 1929 there were 32,000 in New York.

Bootleggers and smugglers

'BOOTLEGGERS' brought illegal liquor supplies into the cities: rum was smuggled from the West Indies, whisky crossed the river to Detroit from Canada. It was soon big business and big businessmen got involved. Joseph Kennedy, the father of the future president, made a great deal of the Kennedy fortune in the illegal liquor trade. Bootleggers organised themselves into gangs to transport the goods and these gangs became rich and powerful.

Illegal liquor

By the late 1920s most alcohol was made at home in illegal 'stills'. It was known as 'moonshine'. Home-brewed 'bathtub' gin could be made drinkable by adding other ingredients to it. In 1930 282,122 illicit stills were seized by government agents. This home-made alcohol was often deadly and caused serious poisoning or blindness. Alcohol was still needed for some industrial processes and although the government deliberately added poison to industrial alcohol much of it went missing and was resold for drinking. Deaths from alcoholic poisoning went up from 98 in 1920 to 760 in 1926.

Stopping the trade

The profits from bootlegging were so great that many people were willing to risk imprisonment. To stop the trade, the Prohibition Bureau employed between 1500 and 2300 agents for the whole of the USA, about 200,000 square miles each. They were badly paid and it soon became clear that something was wrong when it was discovered that some of them were being taken to work in chauffeur-driven cars. One in twelve agents were sacked for taking bribes. The choice for many agents was either taking a bribe, or being beaten up or murdered by gangsters. However, there were some successful and famous agents such as Izzy Einstein, Moe Smith and Eliot Ness.

Organised crime and corruption

There had been criminal gangs before Prohibition but now their activity and power increased. There were huge profits in booze. Gangsters were making about $2 billion a year from it. Rival gangs fought each other to supply the speakeasies with illegal alcohol, hijacking each other's booze supplies and murdering the opposition. Police were bribed to turn a blind eye. Between 1926 and 1927 there were 130 gangland murders in Chicago, for which no one was ever convicted. By the end of the decade, only the most powerful gangs had survived. Cars and Thompson sub-machine guns helped gangsters to run their trade successfully across entire states. Increasingly, organised crime bought its way into government, businesses and trade unions.

One of the worst legacies of Prohibition was the level of corruption it introduced to American society. This included not only Prohibition agents and the police, but also judges and local and state government officials. The bribes were high, and some thought there was not much wrong with people having a drink. But once the bribes were taken, officials were in the pocket of the gangsters for good. This meant that other 'rackets' like protection and prostitution could be run without interference from the police and courts. Corruption extended to the federal government where even some of President Harding's advisers were involved. George Remus, the 'king of the bootleggers', paid thousands of dollars to top government officials for protection from prosecution.

SOURCE 1 Visiting a speakeasy during Prohibition

SOURCE 2 An illegal alcohol still in the 1920s

SOURCE 3 A woman shows how she carries her drink concealed in a special garment under her skirt. You could get gin by calling a telephone number and for $2 a bottle it would be delivered

1. Make a list of the main consequences of Prohibition.
2. Do you think the supporters of Prohibition would have been pleased by these?
3. How did Prohibition encourage Americans to break the law?

SOURCE 4 'Two-gun' Hart was an extremely successful Prohibition agent who made numerous arrests in Montana. What was strange about Hart was that he was an Italian immigrant and the brother of gangster Al Capone. Hart was so successful that he was removed from his post. This was probably because he was damaging the business interests of powerful people who had links with the illegal liquor trade

SOURCE 5 E. Mandeville, talking about Detroit in *Outlook Magazine*, 1925

❝ Ten years ago a dishonest policeman was a rarity ... Now the honest ones are pointed out as rarities ... Their relationship with the bootleggers is perfectly friendly. They have to pinch two out of five once in a while, but they choose the ones who are least willing to pay the bribes. ❞

SOURCE 7 A witness to the Wickersham Commission, 1930, set up to investigate the effects of Prohibition

❝ Today there is not any feeling of resentment against them [the racketeers] because they are looked upon as being part of a trade to satisfy a social want ... The people want their liquor. They do not care what chances the other fellow takes so long as they don't take the chance. ❞

SOURCE 8 Elmer Gertz, a Chicago lawyer in the 1920s

❝ You'd go into what seemed to be an ordinary restaurant that served fried chicken and spaghetti. The wine would be served in coffee cups so that if the police raided the place, you'd appear to be drinking coffee, not wine ...

Prohibition taught America disrespect for the law. It taught many people that the pursuit of crime created very profitable careers ... most people felt there was nothing wrong, particularly when they knew the President was serving liquor in the White House. ❞

SOURCE 6 A cartoon from the Prohibition era entitled 'The National Gesture'

SOURCE 9 Victims of the St Valentine's Day Massacre, 1929. The most horrific example of inter-gang violence was this massacre in which seven members of a gang were gunned down by rivals in a garage. This was a turning point. People were finally shocked into action. There were mounting calls for Prohibition to be ended because it was causing so much gang violence

The end of Prohibition

Prohibition was seen as the cause of the violent crime wave which had swept the USA. More and more Americans turned against it. The Association Against the Prohibition Amendment blamed it for the ills of society just as the old Anti-Saloon League had blamed alcohol. Smart society women organised a campaign for an end to Prohibition in the same way as women had originally campaigned for it to be introduced.

The case for change was helped by the onset of the GREAT DEPRESSION. Legalising alcohol could help to create jobs and prosperity. The government could get taxes from alcohol and stop wasting money on enforcement. In the 1932 election, the Democrat Roosevelt stood for an end to Prohibition and he won. The 18th Amendment was repealed and Prohibition ended on 5 December 1933 after some 13 years.

SOURCE 10 Anti-Prohibition parade in New York in the 1920s. Marches and demonstrations against Prohibition were held across the USA

SOURCE 11 Pauline Sabin led the women's campaign to end Prohibition

66 *Prohibition has led to more violation of and contempt for the law, to more hypocrisy among private citizens as well as police officers than any other thing in our national life. It is responsible for the greatest organised criminal class in the country ... It is time to replace the present corruption, lawlessness and hypocrisy with honesty.* 99

4. Use Sources 1–6 to explain why:
   a) it was difficult to catch people in the illegal liquor trade
   b) why not many people were arrested and convicted.
5. How do Sources 7–8 suggest that the public supported the bootleggers?
6. Choose the three most important reasons from these sources to explain why Prohibition failed.
7. Use Sources 9–11 to explain why Prohibition law was repealed.

■ TASK

Either
Use this diagram to help you write a short essay setting out the main reasons why Prohibition failed.

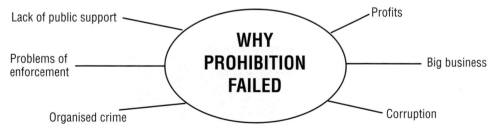

Or
Write a speech campaigning for the end of Prohibition.
Mention:

- why people have not supported Prohibition
- the consequences of Prohibition
- why it's now time to give up 'the noble experiment'.

■ DISCUSSION

'Laws have to be supported by the great majority of the population if they are to work.' Do you agree?

The story of Al Capone

THE STORY OF ALPHONSE 'Scarface' Capone completely captures the role of the gangster in the period of Prohibition. He came from lowly origins, but became extremely rich and powerful by selling illegal alcohol and using violence. He brought the different ethnic gangs in Chicago – Italians, Poles, Irish, Jews and Blacks – under his umbrella organisation to make money out of the illegal liquor trade.

He undertook the systematic corruption of the city of Chicago, buying up policemen, judges and local officials. On polling days, he stationed gunmen on the roofs of polling stations to make sure that people elected the officials on his payroll. By the beginning of the 1930s he virtually controlled the city. He spent over $250,000 to get his own man, Big Bill Thompson, elected mayor.

But Capone became much more than a gangster. He became a star as his photograph on the front cover of *Time* magazine shows. People cheered when he was seen in public. He associated with big businessmen and he organised parties (with alcohol) for them. He opened up clubs and brought in famous artists and jazz musicians such as Louis Armstrong and Duke Ellington. He brought wealth and excitement to Chicago.

He combined violence with charity. He gave generously to the community and some saw him as a kind of Robin Hood. But, in the end, the violence went too far. He was behind the St Valentine's Day Massacre that shocked the American public and led to demands for action to stop the gangster menace.

SOURCE 1 Al Capone in 1930 on the Front cover of *Time* magazine, one of the most influential magazines in the USA

On cover: TIME — The Weekly Newsmagazine — Volume XV — ALPHONSE ("SCARFACE") CAPONE — *A pink apron, a pan of spaghetti.* (See NATIONAL AFFAIRS) — Number 12

SOURCE 2 From a television interview with Doc Cheatham, a jazz musician in Capone's clubs

66 *The city just lit up overnight ... everybody was making money, all this was because of Al Capone. He was selling his beer and whisky to every place in Chicago, even the post office ... there was plenty of this, plenty of that ... everybody was happy. He ruled the city.* 99

SOURCE 3 Milt Hinton, *Memories of Al Capone*

66 *People in Chicago back then looked on Al Capone as a Robin Hood – he helped the poor. My uncle worked for him. He had a dry cleaning and pressing place, and Capone used it as a headquarters for selling alcohol ... Capone sold the alcohol to my uncle for $12 a gallon and we'd sell it to people for $18 a gallon.* 99

Career

- Born 1899 in Brooklyn, New York (parents from southern Italy).
- Joined the Five Points Gang run by 'Terrible Johnny' Torrio.
- In 1919 Capone followed his boss to Chicago, after a short time as a bouncer in a saloon brothel. Torrio and Capone took over other gangs but could not defeat the North Siders.
- In 1925 Torrio was badly injured by 'Bugs' Moran and retired, telling 26-year-old Al: 'It's all yours.' Capone surrounded himself with gangsters he could trust. When he uncovered three of his men plotting against him, he set up a banquet in their honour and at the height of the celebrations used a gift-wrapped club to smash their brains out.
- He brought other gangs under his control and gradually gained political control of Chicago.
- He was behind the St Valentine's Day Massacre in 1929 when rival gangs threatened his operations.
- He escaped jail until 1931 when he was sentenced to eleven years for not paying his income tax. Released in 1939, he never really recovered from his time in the infamous Alcatraz prison.
- Died on 25 January 1947 from natural causes.

Profits of Capone empire

$60 million beer and liquor
$25 m gambling
$10 m protection rackets
$10 m dance halls and prostitution

SOURCE 4 A statement by Al Capone

66 *I make my money by supplying a public demand. If I break the law, my customers, who number hundreds of the best people in Chicago, are as guilty as I am. The only difference between us is that I sell and they buy. Everybody calls me a racketeer. I call myself a businessman. When I sell liquor it's bootlegging. When my patrons serve it on a silver tray on Lake Shore Drive, it's hospitality.* 99

SOURCE 5 F.L. Allen, *Only Yesterday*, 1931

66 *As the profits from beer rolled in, young Capone acquired more finesse ... in the management of politics and politicians. By the middle of the decade he had gained complete control of the suburb of Cicero [in Chicago], had installed his own mayor in office, had posted his agents in the wide-open gambling-resorts and in each of the 161 bars ... he was taking in millions now.* 99

SOURCE 6 Newspaper headlines reporting on the St Valentine's Day Massacre

SOURCE 7 F.L. Allen, *Only Yesterday*, 1931

66 *At half-past ten on the morning of February 14, 1929, seven of the O'Banions were sitting in a garage which went by the name of the S.M.C. Cartage Company, on North Clark Street, waiting for a promised consignment of hijacked liquor. A Cadillac touring-car slid to the curb, and three men dressed as policemen got out, followed by two others in civilian dress. The three supposed policemen entered the garage alone, disarmed the seven O'Banions, and told them to stand in a row against the wall. The victims readily submitted. They were used to police raids and thought nothing of them; they would usually get off easily enough, they expected. But thereupon the two men in civilian clothes emerged from the corridor and calmly mowed down all seven O'Banions with sub-machine gun fire as they stood with hands upraised against the wall. The little drama was completed when the three supposed policemen solemnly marched the two plain-clothes killers across the sidewalk to the waiting car, and all five got in and drove off.* 99

1. Was Prohibition responsible for the rise of Al Capone?
2. What image of Al Capone is presented in Sources 1–4?
3. What does Capone's picture on *Time* magazine (Source 1) tell us?
4. How do Sources 2 and 3 show why he had become popular?
5. Are there any reasons to question the reliability of Sources 2–4 as evidence about Capone?
6. What was the significance of the St Valentine's Day Massacre?

■ TASK

Write a short essay examining the rise and fall of Al Capone and why he is significant in the 1920s.

Were the 1920s a good time for the USA?

■ REVIEW TASK

Look at the people who represent different groups in America:

Wealthy, white businessman

Black farm worker

Worker in a Ford car factory

Young woman – liberated, urban, white

Black jazz musician

Young Italian immigrant

Small-town, white woman

Farmer, with a small amount of land

How do you think they would feel about the 1920s? Write two or three sentences for each person – saying whether the 1920s meant good times or bad times for them, or a mixture of good and bad. What other types of people would you include and what do you think they might say?

■ ACTIVITY

Work in groups to prepare a presentation on the 'Roaring Twenties', focusing on whether these were good times for all Americans. This could take the form of a script for a TV programme or a display to go on the wall. Points to include:

■ why this period was called the Roaring Twenties
■ what exciting new developments and changes were taking place
■ for whom it was a good decade
■ for whom and in what ways it was not a good decade.

3

CRASH AND DEPRESSION

chapter 6

WHAT WERE THE CAUSES AND CONSEQUENCES OF THE WALL STREET CRASH?

What was the Wall Street Crash?

THE ECONOMIC BOOM of the 1920s came to a sudden end in October 1929. In June 1929 prices of stocks and shares had reached new highs. The STOCK MARKET seemed to be a quick and easy way to get rich. More and more people wanted to 'play the market'.

The Wall Street stock market was not regulated. Anybody could buy shares and they could be bought 'on the margin'. This meant, for example, that people could buy $1000 of stock for only $100 and borrow the rest. Buying 'on the margin' became a common practice. People waited for the share prices to go up again and then resold their shares for a profit. It was usually easy to pay back the loan and still make money.

By the summer of 1929 there were 20 million shareholders in America and prices continued to rise. But in October 1929 things began to change. Some people realised that share prices had risen too high and wanted to sell before they fell.

What are shares? Why does the price of shares go up and down?

- Companies borrow money to pay for equipment and staff, etc. They raise this money from investors – people who are prepared to put money into the company. In return, the investors receive shares in the company.
- The investors or 'shareholders' get a share of the profits the company makes. This is called a dividend and is usually paid once a year.
- Shareholders can also sell their shares on the stock market. In the USA the stock market is known as Wall Street.
- The price of shares changes from day to day. If the company is doing well and there is a demand for the shares, then the price will go up.
- But the price can also change, no matter how the company is doing. If a lot of people want to buy the shares the price will go up. If a lot of people start selling the shares and not so many people want to buy them, the price will go down.

The Crash

Saturday, 19 October 1929
3,488,100 shares were bought and sold. There was heavy trading as prices began falling.

Sunday, 20 October 1929
The market was closed. The *New York Times* ran the headline:

'STOCKS DRIVEN DOWN AS WAVE OF SELLING ENGULFS MARKET'

Monday, 21 October 1929
6,091,871 shares changed hands. Prices fell but then went up again as there were still people who wanted to buy shares.

Tuesday, 22 October 1929
Prices rose slightly.

Wednesday, 23 October 1929
Heavy selling of shares in car accessory companies spread to other stocks. In the last hour of trading 2,600,000 shares were sold at ever falling prices. Many people decided that now was the time to get out and sell. Speculators who had bought shares 'on the margin' were told to put up more cash to reduce their loans. But to get the money to do this they had to sell some shares.

'Black' Thursday, 24 October 1929
12,894,650 shares were traded in one day. Prices fell so fast that panic set in and there was a wild scramble to sell. Sometimes no buyer for the shares could be found and prices dived down further.

Wall Street on Thursday, 24 October. A crowd began to form outside the Stock Exchange and police arrived to keep order

Friday, 25 October 1929
At mid-day top bankers met and decided to support the market. Prices steadied and even rose. Richard Whitney (a broker for the huge firm of J.P. Morgan) strolled around buying shares for more than their current price.

Saturday, 26 October 1929
President Herbert Hoover said: 'The fundamental business of the country, that is production and distribution of commodities, is on a sound and prosperous basis.'

BUT

Monday, 28 October 1929
Heavy selling started again. 9,212,800 shares were bought and sold at rapidly falling prices. Three million shares were sold in the last hour of business alone.

Tuesday, 29 October 1929
16,410,030 shares were traded in the worst day in the history of the New York Stock Market. Buyers could not be found at all and panic set in. Shares lost their value and the wealthy, as well as small shareholders, were hit badly.

THE MARKET HAD CRASHED!

S OURCE 2 Carl Sandburg, *The People, Yes*, 1936

 Why when the stock crash came did the man in black silk pyjamas let himself headfirst off a fire escape down ten floors to a stone sidewalk? His sixty million dollars had shrunk to ten million and he didn't see how he could get along.

S OURCE 3 From an interview given by Arthur Robertson, a young businessman at the time of the crash

 A cigar stock at the time (1929) was selling for $115 a share. The market collapsed. The $115 stock dropped to $2 and the company president jumped out of the window of his Wall Street office.

1. Why were share prices so high at the end of 1929?
2. a) What do we mean when we talk about buying shares 'on the margin'?
   b) Why did small investors think it was safe to do this?
3. a) How did the panic selling begin?
   b) How did bankers and politicians try to stop the panic?
   c) Why do you think they gave up after the second wave of selling got under way?
4. What do Sources 1–3 tell us about the effects of the crash on some people?

■ **TASK**

Draw up the front page of a newspaper for the 30 October 1929, the day after the crash. Put on your front page:

■ a suitable heading
■ the story leading up to the crash over the previous ten days
■ stories of personal disaster
■ an article about people 'playing the market' and how this contributed to the crash
■ interviews with people who have lost all their money.

What were the causes of the Wall Street Crash?

AT THE BEGINNING of 1929 the American economy appeared very healthy. But under the surface, it had some major weaknesses and there were also serious problems on the stock exchange. These worked together to bring about the Wall Street Crash.

Weaknesses in the American economy

Many Americans could not afford to buy goods

Overproduction

New mass-production methods and mechanisation meant that production of consumer goods had expanded enormously. In fact, there was overproduction – more was being made than could be consumed. The market was becoming saturated. Those who could afford the goods had bought most of what they wanted. Too many goods were reaching the market, and there were not enough people who could afford to buy them.

Other countries could not afford to buy American goods

Poverty

The new-found wealth of the 1920s was not shared by everyone. Almost 50 per cent of American families had an income of less than $2000 a year – a level which purchased only the bare necessities of life.

Farmers and farm workers
Most of the people who worked in farming were just scraping a living.

Workers
Wages for workers in the old industries remained very low. The smashing of trade unions meant that workers had little power to bargain for better wages.

New immigrants
They were given the lowest-paid jobs.

Blacks
Blacks were discriminated against. Many lived in poverty, both in the rural areas of the South and in northern cities.

Trade

The USA was not able to sell its surplus products to other countries, particularly to Europe, which was a big market. European countries could not afford American goods because:

■ They owed the USA huge amounts of money in war loans and were struggling to pay these back.
■ The US government had put high tariffs on imported goods and American businesses were so strong that European companies could not sell their products to America to earn the dollars to buy American goods.

1. Explain:

■ why there were too many goods on the market
■ why there were not enough people able to buy them
■ which groups of people could not afford to buy goods
■ why the USA could not sell its goods abroad.

Problems on the stock market

From 1921 onwards, the stock market did extremely well because American businesses were so successful. However, from the middle of the 1920s SPECULATION began to increase. People were no longer investing in a company because they thought it was strong. They were simply investing in it in the hope that the price of the shares would rise. And so many people did invest in this way that the price of shares rose out of all proportion to their real value.

AND

People who could ill afford it became involved in speculation. They began to buy stocks and shares with borrowed money ('on the margin'). Their frantic buying helped to push up share prices. But these small investors would not be able to pay back loans to the banks if prices fell.

SO

When, in the autumn of 1929, some experts started to sell shares heavily because they were worried about the weaknesses in the economy and the high share prices, small investors panicked. They saw the fall in prices and rushed to sell their own shares. This led to a complete collapse of prices and thousands of investors lost millions of dollars.

Share prices (in cents)		
	3 March 1928	3 September 1929
Anaconda Can	77	182
Anaconda Copper	54	162
Electric bond and share	90	204
General Electric	129	396
General Motors	140	182
New York Central	160	256
Radio	94	505
United States Steel	138	279
Westinghouse E and M	92	313
Woolworth	181	251

■ TASK

The factors listed below helped to cause the Wall Street Crash.

Decide which are:

- ■ long-term causes
- ■ short-term causes
- ■ immediate causes

A Panic selling of shares in October 1929

B Overproduction in American industry

C No market for US goods in other countries

D Wealth of 1920s not evenly distributed – a very large number of poor Americans

E Speculators playing the market with borrowed money

2. Explain how these factors worked together to bring about the crash.

3. Do you think that speculation on the stock market was the main cause of the Wall Street Crash?

Why did the Wall Street Crash lead to the Great Depression?

THE SHOCK WAVES from the Wall Street Crash were soon felt throughout the American economy and spread quickly throughout the whole world. In America, the crash led to a serious slump in production and was followed by the collapse of the economy, known as the Great Depression. Although the crash played a crucial role in the Depression, the underlying causes of it were the problems in the US economy which we looked at on page 70. The confidence that had helped to create the boom of the 1920s had been shattered.

which we looked at on page 70.

■ DISCUSSION

'Without the Great Crash of 1929 there would have been no Depression in America.' How far do you agree or disagree?

IN THE CITIES

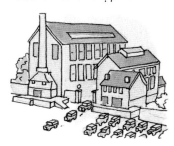
American factories produced cars and consumer goods.

But not enough people could afford them.

So the factories couldn't sell all their goods to Americans.

They couldn't sell them abroad either.

MEANWHILE IN THE COUNTRYSIDE

Farmers produced too much food.

Prices fell.

Farmers and their workers had less money coming in.

Farmers grew even more food to make money.

MEANWHILE IN DOWNTOWN NEW YORK...

The Wall Street Crash of 1929 sent share prices plummeting downwards.

Banks which had invested their customers' money in shares lost a fortune.

The banks called in any outstanding loans to customers.

People lost confidence in the banks and took their money out. Many banks went bust: 659 in 1929, 2294 in 1931.

■ TASK

Draw a flow chart to show how the Wall Street Crash pushed America into the Great Depression. Try drawing it in a spiral (going downwards) to show how things got increasingly worse. You can use the phrases opposite but you have to put them in the right order.

The beginning is done for you:

> After the crash, banks called in loans and there was a fall in demand for goods ...

- ■ The more people unemployed the less money spent on goods.
- ■ Less money spent, so further fall in demand.
- ■ Companies cut back on production/sack workers/pay lower wages.
- ■ More companies go bust, more workers unemployed, further fall in demand and so on.
- ■ Companies go bust, so more unemployed.

Factories cut production . . .

. . . and cut wages . . .

and their work force.

I'll never find another job.

Prices fell lower.

Farmers could not pay debts or mortgages.

The banks took over the farms to pay off the debt.

If you can't pay the mortgage, we'll have to take your farm.

With their loans called in, many companies also went bankrupt. Between 1929 and 1932, 109,371 businesses failed.

More factories closed. By 1932 industrial production in the USA was half that of 1929.

This led to even higher unemployment: 11 million in 1929; 14 million by 1933.

chapter 7

THE EFFECTS OF THE DEPRESSION

H ow did the Depression affect people in the cities?

Unemployment

The most obvious effect of the Depression was the loss of jobs. In industrial areas, mostly the cities of the North and West, unemployment rose rapidly. By 1933 the number out of work had risen to at least 14 million.

Many factory and office workers who had done so well out of the boom of the 1920s lost their jobs. Businesses, hit by falling demand, either laid off workers or reduced their wages. At worst, whole factories were shut down. During the Depression, car production was cut by 80 per cent, and road and building construction fell by 92 per cent. The average hourly wage in the manufacturing industries fell from 59 cents in 1926 to 44 cents in 1933.

Men and women who lost their jobs rarely found other regular work – and unemployment meant poverty. Men would often spend the whole day tramping the streets, looking for work. Any possibility of a job attracted huge queues of men, patiently standing in line – in the vain hope that they would be lucky.

Homelessness

When people lost their jobs, they fell behind with their mortgage repayments. They were forced to sell their homes or hand them over to the banks. Those who fell behind with rent payments were evicted, often violently.

Thousands were taken in by relatives, but a vast number of people had nowhere to go. They ended up on the streets, homeless and destitute. Many lived in shelters made of packing cases and corrugated iron. Others slept on park benches or in warehouses. Some deliberately got themselves arrested because a night in jail meant a bed and some food.

A large number of men (estimated at two million in 1932) travelled from place to place on railway freight wagons, seeking work. Many became tramps, living in tents by the tracks. Thousands of children were to be found living in railcars or close to the railway lines and riding in or under the freight wagons.

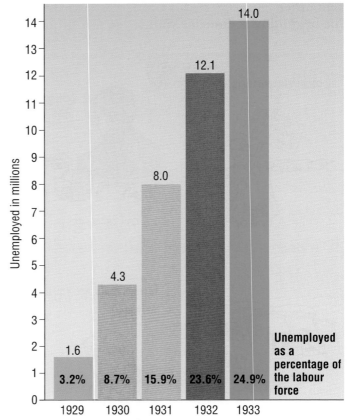

SOURCE 1   Unemployment in the USA, 1929–33

SOURCE 2   The American journalist, Beulah Amidon, described a car factory hit by the Depression in *Toledo: A City the Auto Ran Over, Survey*, 1 March 1930. The vast majority of people in Toledo worked in industries connected with the making of cars

When I was taken through some of the eighty-seven buildings that make up the plant I was reminded of the old desert towns left in the wake of the mining rush. There was the same sense of suspended life, as I moved among silent, untended machines or walked through departments where hundreds of half-finished automobile bodies gathered dust . . .

S OURCE 3 The hungry and homeless queue for Christmas dinner outside the Municipal Lodging House, New York, 25 December 1931

S OURCE 5 One unemployed man's attempt to find work during the Depression

S OURCE 4 Part of the evidence given to a committee of Congress in 1931 by William Foster, leader of the American Communist Party

66 *Thousands of working-class families have been thrown out of their homes because they can no longer pay the rent. In the streets of every large city, workers are dropping, dying and dead from starvation and exposure. Every newspaper reports suicides of these workers, driven to desperation by unemployment and starvation.* 99

1. Look at Source 1.
a) How many people were unemployed in 1929?
b) What proportion of the workforce was this?
c) How had this changed by 1933?
d) In what years did the figures go up fastest?
2. a) What seems to have happened to the car factory in Toledo (Source 2)?
b) Toledo was one of the cities worst hit by the Depression, with almost 80 per cent unemployment. Can you explain why?
3. How reliable do you think the description in Source 4 is? Think about:

■ who wrote it and why he might have written it
■ whether other sources agree or disagree.

4. What did people do to try to get jobs?

S OURCE 6 An apple salesman in New York. There were 6000 men selling apples on the streets of New York in 1932. They also sold ties, vegetables and rubber balls, anything to make a few cents. More than 10,000 of New York's 29,000 manufacturing firms had closed down and one in three of the city's workforce were unemployed

Helping the poor

At this time, America did not have a social security system. There was no unemployment benefit for people who lost their livelihood. There were public RELIEF programmes run by towns and cities which organised temporary homes, clothes, jobs and food. But the scale of the problem meant that these programmes could not provide for everyone and many programmes were cut back as incomes from local taxes fell.

Private charities and wealthy individuals helped. They set up soup kitchens and cheap meals centres to feed the hungry. One-fifth of all children in New York were undernourished; the proportion was higher in mining and other industrial areas.

Self-help

In several cities, groups of unemployed men organised themselves to help poor families and prevent them being evicted from their homes. In Seattle, the unemployed were allowed to pick unmarketable fruit and vegetables by nearby farmers, and to cut timber, which they could use to exchange for services like the doctor. In the coal-mining area of Pennsylvania, unemployed miners dug coal on company property and sold it cheaply. The coal company took them to court but juries refused to convict them.

SOURCE 9 A Hooverville in Seattle, 1934. Shanty-towns of shacks, tents and packing cases grew up on the outskirts of the big cities. These were called Hoovervilles after the President

SOURCE 7 From *New Republic* magazine, February 1933

66 *Last summer in the hot weather, when the smell was sickening and the flies were thick, there were a hundred people a day coming to the dumps ... a widow who used to do housework and laundry, but now had no work at all, fed herself and her fourteen-year-old son on garbage. Before she picked up the meat she would always take off her glasses so that she couldn't see the maggots; but it sometimes made the boy so sick to look at this offal and smell it that he could not bring himself to eat.* 99

SOURCE 10 From *The Grapes of Wrath*, by John Steinbeck, 1939

66 *There was a Hooverville on the edge of every town ... the houses were tents, and weed-thatched enclosures, paper houses, a great junk pile. The man drove his family in and became a citizen of Hooverville – always they were called Hooverville ... If he had no tent, he went to the city dump and brought back cartons and built a house of corrugated paper. And when the rains came the house melted and washed away.* 99

SOURCE 8 A soup kitchen set up to feed unemployed workers. Al Capone provided the money for a soup kitchen to be opened in Chicago

SOURCE 11 From *The Lean Years*, Houghton Mifflin, 1960, recounted by Irving Bernstein

66 *Eleven hundred men standing in a Salvation Army breadline on March 19, 1930, near the Bowery Hotel in Manhattan descended upon two trucks delivering baked goods. Jelly rolls, cookies, rolls and bread were flung into the street with the hungry jobless chasing them. Joseph Drusin of Indiana Township, Pennsylvania, in November 1930 stole a loaf of bread from a neighbour for his four starving children. When caught, Drusin went to the cellar and hung himself.*

By 1932 organised looting of food was a nationwide phenomenon. Helen Hall, a Philadelphia social worker, told a Senate committee that many families sent their children out to steal from wholesale markets, to snatch milk for babies, to lift articles to exchange for food. 99

SOURCE 12 From an article 'Negroes out of Work' in *Nation*, 22 April 1931

66 *The percentage of Negroes among the unemployed runs sometimes four, five, six times as high as their population percentage warrants ... When jobs are scarce preference is given to the white worker in case of a vacancy; but worse than this, a fairly widespread tendency is observed to replace Negro workers with white. White girls have replaced Negro waiters, hotel workers, elevator operators.* 99

5. Why did unemployment lead to widespread poverty and homelessness during the Great Depression?

6. Use Sources 7–12 to give examples of the extent of the poverty.

7. a) What sort of help could the poor get?
   b) Why was this not adequate?

8. How might the President have felt about the name 'Hooverville'? Was this fair to him?

9. Why do you think a gangster like Al Capone set up a soup kitchen like the one shown in Source 8?

10. What does Source 12 suggest about the situation of urban blacks during the Depression?

■ **TASK**

During the Depression some people fell into despair, while others took different forms of action. Use the text and Sources 3–11 to draw up a list of the different ways people coped with or responded to the Depression.

■ **ACTIVITY**

You are a reporter on a New York newspaper in 1932. Your chief has sent you to find out what life is like on the streets for the unemployed. You talk to a variety of people. Using Sources 2–12 in this section, make rough notes in your notebook about the sort of people you have met, what has happened to them, the problems they face, and how they are surviving.

Did the Depression affect all urban Americans?

SOURCE 1 Frederick Lewis Allen, *Only Yesterday*, 1947

66 *One of the strangest things about the Depression was that it was so nearly invisible to the naked eye ... To be sure, the streets were less crowded with trucks than they had been, many shops stood vacant ... and chimneys which should have been smoking were not doing so ... There just didn't seem to be so many people about.* 99

SOURCE 2 The magazine *Fortune* in the winter of 1931–32 had noted that a visitor from out of town would

66 *be surprised to discover that, at first and even at second glance, New York City is much the same as it was in pre-depression days ... Wandering about the city looking for disaster, the visitor will very likely find no more than he would have in New York in any other winter.* 99

SOURCE 3 Studs Terkel, *Hard Times*, 1970. This extract is from an interview with Dr Rossman, a psychiatrist during the 1930s

66 *You wouldn't know a depression was going on ... don't forget that the highest employment was less than 20 per cent.*

[Interviewer] Your patients, then, weren't really affected.

Not very much. They paid reasonable fees. I just came across a handbook that I had between 1931 and 1934, and, by God, I was in those days making $2,000 a month which was a hell of a lot of money. 99

SOURCE 6 Alistair Cooke, *America*, 1973

66 *The Great Depression ... blighted everybody, except the very poor who had nothing to lose ... There were skyscrapers just finished that lacked tenants ... There were truckers with nothing to truck, milk that went undelivered to people who couldn't afford it ... [In 1932] I couldn't go out in the evening to mail a letter without being stopped by nicely dressed men ... cadging dimes and quarters.* 99

SOURCE 7 R. and H. Lynd, *Middletown in Transition*, 1937

66 *The city had been shaken for nearly six years by a catastrophe involving not only people's values but, in the case of many, their very existence ... virtually nobody in the community had been cushioned against the blow; the great knife of the depression had cut down impartially through the entire population, cleaving open the lives and hopes of the rich as well as the poor.* 99

SOURCE 4 On the whole, the rich remained rich during the Depression. Some wealthy people did lose everything in the Wall Street Crash, but most, like multi-millionaire John D. Rockerfeller, pictured above, held their wealth in a variety of assets such as gold and property

SOURCE 5

Year	Personal consumption expenditure ($ billions)
1929	128.1
1930	120.3
1931	116.6
1932	106.0
1933	103.5
1934	108.9
1935	115.8

1. What do Sources 1–4 suggest about the impact of the Depression on all Americans?
2. How is this supported by the figures in Source 5?
3. What different view of the Depression is suggested by Sources 6 and 7?
4. How can you account for these different views? What general conclusions can you come to?

How did the Depression affect people in the countryside?

MANY FARMERS, as we have seen, did not share in the prosperity of the 1920s. Could life get any worse for them during the Great Depression?

As the Depression hit town and country, people struggled to buy even basic goods such as food and clothing. Farmers found they could not sell their produce. Prices fell so low that farmers could not even afford to harvest their crops. Wheat and fruit were allowed to rot, and farm animals were killed instead of being taken to market.

As their income fell, more and more farmers went bankrupt and were evicted by the banks.

SOURCE 1 In 1932, Oscar Ameringer gave evidence before a sub-committee of the House of Representatives

66 *During the last three months I have visited . . . some 20 states of this wonderfully rich and beautiful country. A number of Montana citizens told me of thousands of bushels of wheat left in the fields uncut on account of its low price that hardly paid for the harvesting. In Oregon I saw thousands of bushels of apples rotting in the orchards. At the same time there are millions of children who, on account of the poverty of their parents, will not eat one apple this winter.*

While I was in Oregon, the Portland Oregon *[local newspaper] bemoaned the fact that thousands of ewes were killed by the sheep raisers because they did not bring enough in the market to pay freight on them . . . I saw men picking for meat scraps in the garbage cans of the cities of New York and Chicago. I talked to one man in a restaurant in Chicago . . . He said that he had killed 3,000 sheep this fall and thrown them down the canyon because it cost $1.10 to ship a sheep and then he would get less than a dollar for it. He said he could not afford to feed the sheep and he would not let them starve so he just cut their throats and threw them down the canyon.*

The farmers are being pauperised [made poor] by the poverty of industrial populations and the industrial populations are being pauperised by the poverty of the farmers. Neither has the money to buy the product of the other; hence we have overproduction and under-consumption at the same time. 99

1. How did the Depression in the towns make life much harder for farmers?
2. What do Sources 1–5 tell you about the effect of the Depression in the countryside?
3. How does Source 1 explain why so many people were going hungry when there was so much food available?

SOURCE 2 A poor farming family outside their log cabin home in Wisconsin, 1937

SOURCE 3 Eskine Calder was a radical writer who hated the American capitalist system. Here he writes in the *New York Post* newspaper in 1935. He is describing a family in Georgia who had had no food for three days, when one of the men turned up with a small amount of meat and cornmeal

     66 *A six-year-old boy licked the paper bag the meat had been brought in. His legs were scarcely any larger than a medium sized dog's leg and his belly was as large as that of a 130-pound woman's. Suffering from rickets and anaemia, his legs were unable to carry him for more than a dozen steps at a time; suffering from malnutrition, his belly was swollen several times its normal size. His face was bony and white. He was starving to death.*

     In the other room of the house, without chairs, beds, or tables, a woman lay rolled up in some quilts trying to sleep. On the floor before an open fire lay two babies, neither a year old, sucking the dry teats of a mongrel bitch. **99**

SOURCE 4 Howard Zinn, *A People's History of the United States*, 1980

     66 *The effects of the Depression could force normally law-abiding citizens to take desperate measures:*

     ... she walked into the local store, asked for a 24-pound sack of flour, gave it to her little boy to take it outside, then filled a sack of sugar and said to the storekeeper, 'Well, I'll see you in ninety days. I have to feed some children ... I'll pay you, don't worry.' And when he objected, she pulled out her pistol (which as a midwife travelling alone through the hills, she had a permit to carry) and said 'Martin, if you try to take this grub away from me, God knows if they electrocute me for it tomorrow, I'll shoot you six times in a minute.' **99**

4. Some historians might say that the writer of Source 3 has chosen an exaggerated case, even if true, to make his point.
a) Why might they say this?
b) How far do the other sources support Source 3?
5. Why do you think the Depression hit black farmers and labourers harder than whites?

SOURCE 5 Black sharecroppers. Black farmers and agricultural labourers were often worse off than their white neighbours. They usually lost their land and jobs first

The Dust Bowl

THE DEPRESSION MADE it hard for poor farmers to earn a living – and then came the Dust Bowl. Between 1930 and 1936 the South and Midwest suffered a serious drought. The area had once been animal grazing land but during the First World War farmers were encouraged to change to arable farming and to grow crops that could be sold abroad. This continued after the war.

By 1930 much of the land had been overfarmed and was already losing its fertility. Then came year after year of hot summers, driving wind and little rainfall. Without its grass covering, the top soil turned to dust and the wind whipped the dust into storms which smothered everything in sight. By 1936, over 20 million hectares of land in Kansas, Oklahoma, Texas, New Mexico and Colorado had become like a desert. Thousands of farmers were ruined.

SOURCE 1 Farmland turned to dust by overfarming and drought, Dallas, 1936

SOURCE 2 George Greenfield, *Readers Digest*, May 1937

66 The Dust Bowl is a dying land ... I have not seen more than two automobiles on the road that parallels the railroad track for a hundred miles or more. I have seen human beings only when passing bleak villages, consisting of a few shacks. Houses empty, yards empty. I have not seen a single child in these ghost-like, pathetic villages. The few people I saw looked like lost people living in a lost land.

I do not exaggerate when I say that in this country there is now no life for miles upon miles; no human beings, no birds, no animals. Only a dull brown land with cracks showing. Hills furrowed with eroded gullies – you have seen pictures like that in ruins of lost civilisations. 99

SOURCE 3 From *Letters from the Dust Bowl*, by Carolyn Henderson

66 Wearing our shade hats, with the handkerchiefs tied over our faces and vaseline in our nostrils, we have been trying to rescue our home from the wind-blown dust which penetrates wherever air can go. It is an almost hopeless task, for there is rarely a day when at some time the dust clouds do not roll over. 'Visibility' approaches zero and everything is covered again with a silt-like deposit which may vary in depth from a film to actual ripples on the kitchen floor. I keep oiled cloths on the window sills and between the upper and lower sashes. They help just a little to keep back or collect the dust. Some seal the windows with the gummed paper strips used in wrapping parcels, but no method is fully effective ...

Few residents have left our neighbourhood, but on a sixty-mile trip yesterday we saw ... little abandoned homes where people had drilled deep wells for the precious water, had set vines, built reservoirs, and fenced in gardens – and now everything walled in or half buried by banks of drifted soil told a painful story of loss and disappointment. 99

1. What caused the Dust Bowl?
2. Use Sources 1–3 to describe how people who lived in the Dust Bowl were affected.
3. Why are eye-witness accounts like those in Sources 2 and 3 so valuable to historians?
4. If you were a government official in the areas affected by the Dust Bowl, what advice would you give to farmers?

Migrants

IN THE 1920s, farmers from the South and Midwest had started to move away, in search of work and better land to farm. During the 1930s, as the dust storms destroyed what was left of the land, many more packed their few belongings and began the long journey to what they hoped was the land of plenty – California.

Many of the farmers came from Oklahoma and Arkansas, which had been particularly badly affected by the drought. When they reached California, the 'Okies' and 'Arkies' often found they did not receive a warm welcome.

SOURCE 1 Migrants camping on road as they made the journey to California

SOURCE 2 John Steinbeck, *The Grapes of Wrath*, 1939

66 *They streamed over the mountains, hungry and restless as ants, scurrying to find work to do – to lift, to push, to pull, to pick, to cut – anything, any burden to bear for food. The kids are hungry. We've got no place to live. Like ants scurrying for work and most of all for land ... They were hungry and they were fierce. And they hoped to find a home, and they found only hatred.* 99

SOURCE 3 Map showing migration

■ TASK

Use the sources and information here and in the section on the Dust Bowl to explain:

■ why so many farmers and farm workers left their homes
■ where they were going
■ how they got there
■ what sort of reception they were likely to find.

SOURCE 4 A sign on the Californian border, 1935

82

The Grapes of Wrath

The extracts below are all taken from John Steinbeck's novel *The Grapes of Wrath*, 1939. Steinbeck spent months living with migrants in California. The magazine *Life* commented, 'never before had the facts behind a great work of fiction been so carefully researched.' Other critics have said the book is hopelessly romantic and exaggerated in its treatment of the main characters.

The book tells the story of the Joad family – Ma and Pa, Grampa and Granma, Uncle John and several children including Tom, Ruthie, Winfield and Rose of Sharon – who travelled from Oklahoma to California looking for a new start.

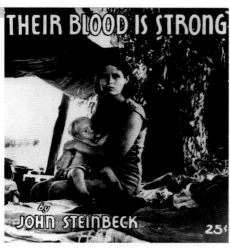

The road

> 66 *Highway 66 is the main migrant road ... The people in flight streamed out on 66, sometimes in a single car, sometimes a little caravan. All day they rolled slowly along the road, and at night they stopped near water. In the day, ancient leaky radiators sent up columns of steam, loose connecting rods hammered and pounded.... 'F we can on'y get to California where the oranges grow before this here ol'jub blows up. 'F we on'y can ...' 99*

The journey

The long, hot journey was too much for Grampa. He died and was buried by the side of the road. They put a note in a fruit jar with the body:

> 66 *'This here is William James Joad, dyed [died] of a stroke, old, old man. His folks buried him because they got no money to pay for funerls [funerals]. Nobody kilt [killed] him. Just a stroke and he dyed.' 99*

Granma Joad became increasingly ill as they approached California but they had to cross a desert at night to get there – and they did not dare stop in case the truck broke down. Granma died just before they had crossed the state line into California.

> 66 *Suddenly they saw the great valley below them ... the vineyards, the orchards, the great flat valley, green and beautiful ... the grainfields golden in the morning, and the willow lines, the eucalyptus trees in rows ... The peach trees and the walnut groves, and the dark green patches of oranges ... Ruthie and Winfield scrambled down from the car, and they stood silent and awestruck ... and Ruthie whispered: 'It's California.' 99*

SOURCE 5 This photo of a migrant mother and child was used as the cover of an earlier Steinbeck novel. Steinbeck was deeply fascinated by this and other photos of the Depression. You can find out more about these photos on pages 85–87

Work

Getting work was difficult because there were so many migrants desperate to earn money. The Californian employers took advantage of this.

> 66 *The car door opened and a man got out ... The man said: 'You men want work?' ... One of the squatting men spoke at last. 'Sure we wanta work. Where's the work?' 'Tulare county. Fruit's opening up. Need a lot of pickers.' 99*

The men asked him to give them a signed contract but the man hiring labour wouldn't.

> 66 *Floyd said: 'Twice now I've fell for that. Maybe he needs a thousan' men. He'll get five thousan' there, an' he'll pay fifteen cents an hour. An' you poor bastards'll have to take it 'cause you'll be hungry. 'F he wants to hire men, let him hire 'em an' write it out an' say what he's gonna pay.'*
>
> *The contractor turned to the Chevrolet and called to his companion: 'This fella. He's talkin' red, agitating trouble ... Ever seen 'im before' ...*
>
> *'Hmm, seems I have. Las' week when that used-car lot was busted into. Seems like I seen this fella hangin' aroun' ... 'Get in that car,' he said, and he unhooked the strap that covered the butt of his automatic.*
>
> *Tom said: 'You got nothin' on him.'*
>
> *The deputy swung around, 'F you's like to go in too, you jus' open your trap once more ' ...*
>
> *The contractor turned back to the men. 'You fellas don't want to listen to these goddamn reds. Trouble-makers – they'll get you in trouble. Now I can use all of you in Tulare county.' 99*

In a government camp

The Joads moved from camp to camp looking for work, but had little luck. Eventually, they arrived at a government camp.

> *Ma demanded: 'You got wash-tubs – running water?'*
>
> *'Sure.'*
>
> *'Oh! Praise God,' said Ma . . .*
>
> *The watchman looked up . . . 'the camp site costs a dollar a week, but you can work it out, carrying garbage, keeping the camp clean – stuff like that . . . there's five sanitary units. Each one elects a Central Committee man. Now that committee makes the laws. What they say goes'. . .*
>
> *[Tom] 'You mean to say the fellas that runs the camp is jus' fellas – campin' here?'*
>
> *'Sure, and it works . . . Then there's the ladies. They keep care of kids an' look after the sanitary units. If your ma isn't working, she'll look after kids for the ones that is working . . . and a nurse comes out an' teaches 'em . . . '*
>
> *[Tom] 'Well for Christ's sake! Why ain't they more places like this?'*

Starvation amidst plenty

As in other areas of agriculture, too much fruit was being produced and a lot of it was thrown away while people went hungry.

> *The works of the roots of the vine, of the trees, must be destroyed to keep up the price, and this is the saddest, bitterest thing of all. Car-loads of oranges dumped on the ground . . . and men with hoses squirt kerosene on the oranges . . . A million people hungry, needing the fruit – and kerosene sprayed over the golden mountain . . .*
>
> *[And the men] dump potatoes in the rivers and place guards along the banks to keep the hungry people from fishing them out, slaughter the pigs and bury them . . .*
>
> *There is a crime here that goes beyond denunciation . . . children dying of pellagra must die because a profit cannot be taken from an orange. And coroners must fill in the certificates – died of malnutrition – because the food must be forced to rot . . . and in the eyes of the hungry there is a growing wrath. In the souls of the people the grapes of wrath are filling and growing heavy.*

What happened to the Joads

The Joads go through hard times finding little help and much intolerance and cruelty, moving from place to place in search of work. The end of the book sees them no better off – caught in a flood, the baby of Rose of Sharon stillborn – but they still have hope and faith in themselves to get through.

SOURCE 6 A migrant family on the road, looking for work, 1938

1. What have you learnt from the extracts about:

    ■ the Joad family's journey to California
    ■ how the Californian land owners treated the Okies
    ■ what the government migrant camps were like
    ■ the method of keeping up agricultural prices.

2. Is John Steinbeck's novel good historical evidence or not?

    Write your answer after you have thought about these questions:

    ■ Was the novel based on good knowledge of the migrants?
    ■ Why do you think Steinbeck wrote the novel?
    ■ Is there any reason why he might have made things appear worse than they were?
    ■ What parts of the book might be useful even if the story is fictional?

3. Do you think that what you learned from the extracts (question 1) is what it was really like? Explain your answer.

Documentary photographs of the Depression

THE MOST POWERFUL images of America in the 1930s are represented in the photographs from this period. Many of these were commissioned as a documentary record. The Farm Security Administration (FSA) set up a photographic unit to record the effects of the Depression in the American countryside.

Some of the most famous photographs were taken by Dorothea Lange and Walker Evans. Lange was hired by the state authorities of California to take photos of the migrant farm workers who had moved into the state (see also the photographs on pages 82–84). Many books of documentary photographs were published. One of the most well known is *Let us Now Praise Famous Men* by Walker Evans.

SOURCE 1
Migrant mother with her children, Nipomo, California, 1936, photographed by Dorothea Lange

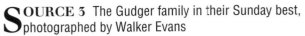

SOURCE 3 The Gudger family in their Sunday best, photographed by Walker Evans

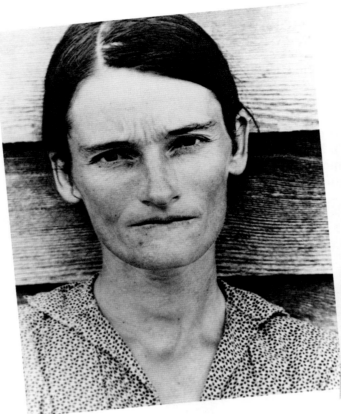

SOURCE 2 Annie Mae Gudger, a sharecropper wife, photographed by Walker Evans

SOURCE 4 The Rickettses, a sharecropper family, photographed by Walker Evans

SOURCE 5 William Stott, *Documentary Expression and Thirties America*, 1973

" *American documentary photographs of the 1930s had a romantic view. They come to us only in images meant to break our heart. Never are they vicious, never responsible for their misery. And this, of course, was intentional. The people shown have 'simple dignity'; they have 'leaned against the wind and worked in the sun and owned their own land'. They are honest, straight-standing and decent . . .*

When taking photographs, Bourke-White looked for 'faces that would express what we wanted to tell'. But it was not just certain faces she sought . . . it was a certain expression.

[It might take an hour before] she got from her subjects the look she wanted. The look: mournful, plaintive, nakedly near tears . . .

Most documentary photographs of the 1930s were not intentionally deceptive . . . but all prejudiced their evidence in selecting it. "

SOURCE 6 Stott makes this point about the value of the photographs

" *Lange's noble pictures of the Dust Bowl – an abandoned shack floating in a sea of tractor furrows that rise even to the porch – explain completely why no humans are to be seen and what has pushed them out. The photographs of deserted Western Roads running straight ahead through nowhere to the blurred horizon make the viewer know, as Roy Stryker said, 'what it would feel like to be an actual witness of the scene'.* "

SOURCE 7 Abandoned farm house in Texas, 1938, photographed by Dorothea Lange

Look carefully at the photographs in Sources 1–4 and 7, and read Sources 5 and 6 before answering the questions. Refer to them in your answers.

1. Why were these photographs taken?
2. Do you think they were carefully posed? Explain your answer, referring to the photographs and Source 5.
3. How does Annie Mae Gudger look in Source 2 compared with how she looks in Source 3 (she is top right)?
4. Why do you think Source 3 was not used in the documentary books of the time?
5. Why is the selection of certain shots and photographs so important when considering their use as historical evidence?
6. What is the value of these photographs to people who want to learn about poverty in rural America in the 1930s? Read Source 6 again before you answer this.

■ **ACTIVITY**

You are a photo-journalist in 1937. This means that you use photographs to tell stories in magazines. Your Editor has asked you to do a feature on the effects of the Depression. However, she has only allowed you space for four photographs. Choose four photographs from pages 75–87 that you think best sum up the effects of the Depression on people in the cities and in the countryside. For each one, write long captions that explain the circumstances which the photographs are representing. You must also give your Editor reasons why you chose them and not the others.

Why were the 1930s a golden age for Hollywood?

The 1930s are known as the Golden Age of Hollywood. Sound arrived in 1929. By the end of the 1930s colour film had too. During the 1930s film productions became more lavish and expensive. Throughout the Depression 60 to 100 million people went to the cinema every week. That's almost half the population of the USA! Why?

A night out at the Picture Palace

You are walking down Main Street, Smalltown. It is 1933. The shops look dreary these days. You used to be able to buy anything on Main Street – a car, a tractor, a new hat, a set of encyclopaedias. But half the shops have closed because of the Depression. The rest have cut back.

A man on the sidewalk asks you for money as you go by. He mutters about having no job, no food, and a wife and child to support. You have a dollar in your pocket but you ignore him. You have other plans for your dollar. You are going to the Picture Palace. There it is at the end of the street – the biggest building on Main Street. It is also the grandest with its spires, sculptures and bright lights. It's like something straight out of Hollywood itself. While the rest of the town is struggling, the Picture Palace is booming. Even now, there is a queue outside. They change the film every two days. Some people go two or three times a week.

Your ticket costs you just 25 cents – less than a loaf of bread – but it buys you two hours of luxury. You climb up a sweeping staircase from the box office. An usher shows you to your seat. This is the closest you are ever going to get to a real palace. Satin curtains draw back to reveal a massive screen. Chandeliers dim. You sink back into your comfortable seat as an overwhelming sound erupts from the speakers each side of the cinema and dozens of beautiful women, wearing only skimpy silk, emerge out of the misty set towards you. One by one, they pirouette their way down a great staircase towards a tumbling stream and swimming pool. This is the latest Busby Berkeley musical, *Footlight Parade*.

You've seen a dozen films like it this year. Every musical is more sumptious than the last. The story is always simple – a young dancer desperate for a break gets her chance when the talentless, arrogant and overpaid star of the show flounces out in a fit of rage. The young dancer of course takes her place, achieves instant fame and wealth, and gets the man of her dreams into the bargain. If only something like that could happen to you ... It all helps to lift those Depression blues.

The credits roll and the film is over. Back out into the real world again? Afraid so! But you can take a part of this fantasy world home with you. At the door they are selling *Movie Magazine* and you buy a copy with the rest of your dollar. It has a story called 'At home with Ruby Keeler'. There's Ruby living like a queen in her luxurious mansion yet smiling innocently at you. You will pin that picture on your wall at home, alongside mysterious Greta Garbo, dashing Errol Flynn, sexy Marlene Dietrich, and romantic Gary Cooper.

■ ACTIVITY

You are the manager of the Smalltown Picture Palace. Plan out a poster advertising your cinema. What are its real attractions in Depression time?

1. How was a trip to the cinema in the 1930s similar to or different from a trip to the cinema today?
2. Why do you think Busby Berkeley musicals were so successful and popular during the Depression?
3. Here are some other types of films which were very popular in the 1930s. For each type, explain why they might be attractive to someone suffering the effects of the Depression:

   ■ **gangster movies**, for example, *Little Caesar* – a young man starts with nothing, then gains massive wealth and power through violence and intimidation,
   ■ **monster movies**, for example, *Frankenstein* – a dreadful uncontrollable monster is created by an irresponsible scientist
   ■ **romantic comedies**, for example, *It Happened One Night* – a rich heiress falls in love with a hard-up journalist.

4. Complete a table like the one opposite to explain how each factor helped to make the 1930s a golden age for Hollywood.

SOURCE 1 A still from the Busby Berkeley movie, *Footlight Parade*, 1933

SOURCE 2 The cover of a movie magazine called *Screen Book* which was sold during the 1930s. These magazines encouraged the public's worship of movie stars

Factors	How it helped
a improved technology	
b the star system	
c movie magazines	
d the impact of the Depression	
e the films themselves	
f the cinemas	

5. Which do you think was the most important factor in the success of Hollywood in the 1930s?
6. Many of the films of the 1930s can still be seen today. Explain how these films are useful/not useful as historical evidence about the 1930s.

chapter 8

WHY WAS FRANKLIN D. ROOSEVELT ELECTED PRESIDENT IN 1932?

What action did Hoover's government take to deal with the Depression?

WHEN THE DEPRESSION began, President Hoover took the view that it would not last long and that the country would soon return to prosperity.

However, as more people lost their jobs and as poverty mounted, he realised that the government would have to do something.

Hoover has been accused of doing nothing about the Depression. This is not true. By 1932 his government had started to take some action, as the diagram below shows. But was it too little too late?

The Farm Board
To help farmers, the Board bought surplus farm produce to keep prices up. But it had little effect because the slide in prices was so great and the Board did not have enough money.

Hoover offered no real solution to the falling demand for goods.

People not buying manufactured goods. Businesses collapsing or cutting back on production and staff

Food prices falling. Farmers' incomes very low

Relief
Hoover did not believe that the federal government should provide relief for the hungry and homeless. He saw this as the responsibility of local state governments and charities. But the state governments did not have enough money.

Government schemes
The government provided $423 million for a building programme to provide new jobs, e.g. the Hoover Dam on the Colorado River. This was a step in the right direction, but far more money was needed to provide a greater number of jobs.

People hungry and homeless. Need help and jobs

PROBLEMS OF THE DEPRESSION

Can't sell manufactured goods to foreign countries

Hawley-Smoot Act, 1930
In 1930 the Hawley-Smoot Act was passed which increased customs duties on a wide range of imported foodstuffs and manufactured items, by 50 per cent. The government hoped that this would encourage people to buy cheaper American-made goods. However, few people could afford goods whether they were produced at home or abroad. Foreign countries retaliated by taxing American goods, so trade fell even further.

Employers paying low wages. Workers have no money to buy goods

Businesses failing because banks won't lend them money. More unemployed

Voluntary agreements
Hoover encouraged employers to make voluntary agreements with their workforce to keep wages up and production steady, but these did not work.

The Reconstruction Finance Corporation, 1932
This provided loans totalling $1500 million to businesses in order to help them to get back on their feet.

1. Why was Hoover's government accused of not doing enough to deal with the problems of the Depression?

Protest – was America on the brink of revolution?

AS HOOVER'S GOVERNMENT appeared to be doing little to help those suffering from the Depression, frustration mounted. Protest turned to violence. In 1930, a rally of the unemployed in New York turned into a riot as police charged the crowd. It was not only the unemployed who were protesting. Workers in employment were sick of the starvation level wages they were paid. This led to strikes and bitter clashes in many American cities.

In the countryside, farmers refused to let food into towns like Sioux City in Iowa until they were paid enough for their produce. Roads were blockaded, fights broke out, and trains and cars were stopped. Hoover was likened to Louis XVI (the king executed in the French Revolution), and the actions of the farmers to the Boston Tea Party (during the American Revolution in 1776).

Bonus Marchers

The biggest show of discontent was the 'Bonus March' of 1932. At the end of the First World War, the surviving soldiers had been promised a 'bonus' or pension that would be paid to them in 1945. The veterans now called on the government to pay the bonus early because they desperately needed the money. Some 15,000, many with their wives and children, streamed into Washington and set up camp in tents and temporary homes.

Hoover refused to give in to such demonstrations and the Bonus Marchers were accused of being communists and criminals. There was talk that this might lead to revolution if it was not controlled. Hoover called in the army led by General MacArthur. The Bonus Marchers were dispersed by armed troops, tanks and tear gas. Their tents were set on fire. Two babies died of tear gas, and many people including children were injured. The Bonus Marchers were forced out of Washington but the actions of the army made Hoover even more unpopular.

SOURCE 1   Police attacking the Bonus Marchers, 1932

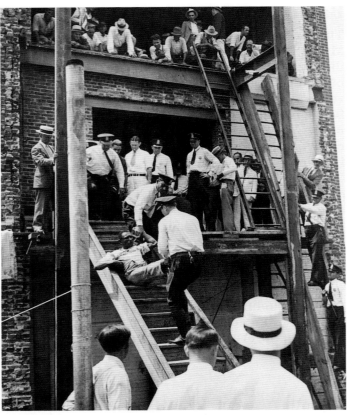

SOURCE 2 A veteran being pulled out of a building by police during the Bonus March

1. a) How does General MacArthur account for his actions against the 'Bonus Army' (Source 4)?
   b) Is he a reliable witness?
2. Why do you think many Americans, like the writer of Source 5, were ashamed by the way Hoover dealt with the Bonus Marchers?
3. The government put down demonstrations and protests with strong action and sometimes violence. What effect do you think this might have on the people involved in them and on other people who supported them?

SOURCE 3 William Green, moderate trade union leader, *Time*, 19 October 1931

❝ No social order is secure where wealth flows at such a rate into the hands of the few away from the many ... I warn the people who are exploiting the workers that they can only drive them so far before they will turn on them and destroy them! They are taking no account of the history of nations in which governments have been overturned. Revolution grows out of the depths of hunger. ❞

SOURCE 4 General Douglas MacArthur on the 'Bonus Army' he expelled from Washington in July 1932, from *The Memoirs of Herbert Hoover, The Great Depression 1919–1941*, 1953

❝ That mob was a bad looking mob. It was animated by the essence of revolution. The gentleness, the consideration, with which they had been treated had been mistaken for weakness and they came to the conclusion, beyond a shadow of a doubt, that they were about to take over in some arbitrary way whether by direct control of the Government or else to control it by indirect methods. It is my opinion that had the President not acted today, had he permitted this thing to go on for 24 hours more, he would have been faced with a grave situation which would have caused a real battle. Had he let it go on another week I believe the institutions of our Government would have been very severely threatened. ❞

SOURCE 5 Political commentator after the Bonus Marchers had been cleared out

❝ Never before in this country has a government fallen to so low a place in popular estimation or been so universally an object of cynical contempt. Never before has [a president] given his name so freely to latrines and offal dumps, or had his face banished from the [cinema] screen to avoid the hoots and jeers of children. ❞

SOURCE 6 John Simpson, President of the National Farmers Union, warned the Senate in January 1933

❝ The biggest and finest crop of revolutions is sprouting all over the country right now. ❞

SOURCE 7 President of the Farmers' Union of Wisconsin speaking to a Senate committee, 1932

❝ Farmers are just ready to do anything to get even with the situation ... I honestly believe that if some of them could buy airplanes they would come down here to Washington to blow you fellows up ... The farmer is a naturally conservative individual, but you cannot find a conservative farmer today. Any economic system that has in its power to set me and my wife in the streets, at my age – what can I see but red? ❞

4. a) What are the warnings being given in Sources 3, 6 and 7?

b) What could these men gain by giving exaggerated warnings?

c) How reliable are their judgements as evidence of the state of feeling amongst farmers and workers?

5. a) Why does the writer of Source 8 think the workers will rise up in revolution?

b) Why might you be careful about accepting this source as reliable?

6. What is Irving Bernstein's view in Source 9?

SOURCE 8 William Z. Forster, chairman of the American Communist Party, speaking to a Congress House committee in late 1930

❝ The bloody path that capitalism is travelling today over the lives of the workers is conclusive proof that ... the capitalists will use their last gun and their last dollar in defense of the only principle they ever held sacred – that is, the unrestricted right to make a profit out of the misery of the masses ... The Communist Party prepares the working class to carry out in the proletarian [workers'] revolution, that principle announced in the Declaration of Independence: 'It is the right, it is the duty', of the working masses to throw off such government. ❞

SOURCE 9 Irving Bernstein, *The Lean Years*, 1960

❝ Despite momentary success ... the communist program amongst the unemployed was a failure. Its principal achievement was to raise relief standards in some communities ... The real aim – the organisation of the jobless for revolution – did not come to pass. In fact, the unemployed had much shorter goals: relief and jobs. Their obsession with survival made them bad material for revolution ... The writers who toured the nation in search of revolution confirmed this conclusion. ❞

■ TASK

1. Statements A–C in the table below give three possible outcomes to America's situation in 1932. Rate each statement:

- ■ not likely
- ■ likely
- ■ very likely

by putting a tick in the appropriate column.

	not likely	likely	very likely
A America was heading towards a very difficult time when there might be violence.			
B America was just going through a difficult patch and the government would have no trouble in keeping control.			
C America was heading towards a revolution.			

2. Explain your answers to question 1 above and discuss the problems of America at the end of 1932. Think about:

- ■ the government's actions to deal with the Depression
- ■ the government's response to protest
- ■ the feelings of the people
- ■ what could happen even if a revolution was unlikely.

Or

3. Write an article for *Time* magazine. In it you could argue:

a) that America is facing a massive outbreak of violence and possibly revolution. Call it 'America on the brink of revolution'.

or

b) that, although the government is disliked and there is a strong protest movement, there is no real likelihood of revolution. Call it 'Talk of revolution is all hot air'.

The 1932 election

IN 1932, in the depths of the Depression, there was a Presidential election. The two candidates were Herbert Hoover and Franklin D. Roosevelt.

Herbert Hoover

Born in 1874, Hoover lost both parents before he was eleven years old. He was brought up by uncles and became an office boy on leaving school. At eighteen he went to university. He worked hard and became a respected and wealthy mining engineer.

By the age of 40 he was a multi-millionaire and decided to go into politics. After the First World War, Hoover did a good job helping to feed Europe's starving. As Secretary of Commerce in the 1920s, he had been an important figure in the government and the Republican Party.

Hoover had been the clear choice for Republican candidate in the 1928 election. He had won on the promise of continued prosperity and the final triumph over poverty. He said that every American home would have 'two cars in every garage and a chicken in the pot'.

Hoover believed in self-help and 'rugged individualism', that is, that individuals could achieve success through their own effort and hard work (as he had done).

Campaign 1932

Hoover promised that the great 'turnaround' would happen soon and prosperity would return. He said that businesses would bring about an end to the Depression if they were left alone. It was not the government's job to interfere.

But many Americans blamed Hoover for the mess they were in. A famous banner carried in a demonstration of Iowa farmers said: 'In Hoover we trusted and now we are busted'. People felt that Hoover was not doing anything to get America out of the Depression.

Hoover believed that relief should be provided by local government and private charities, not the government. He thought too much help would damage the spirit of self-reliance that had made America great.

His attitude made people think that he was cold and uncaring. This is why the shanty towns for the homeless were called 'Hoovervilles' and the newspapers they slept in were 'Hoover blankets'.

Hoover v

SOURCE 1 President Hoover making a speech on Armistice Day, 1929

1. Look at Source 1. How is President Hoover trying to show his love of his country?
2. Look at Source 2.
a) Why was this photograph of Roosevelt usually cropped cut short just below his knees before being published in the newspapers?
b) If uncut photographs like this had been printed during the election campaign, do you think it would have affected the way people voted?

Roosevelt

SOURCE 2 Roosevelt pictured after he had won the 1932 election

3. Draw a chart like the one below. On the left-hand side, list the factors working in favour of Roosevelt. These can include positive points about him and negative points about Hoover. Do the same for Hoover on the right-hand side.

Points in favour of Roosevelt	Points in favour of Hoover

Franklin D. Roosevelt

Franklin Delano Roosevelt, or FDR as he is often called, came from a very different background to Hoover. Born in 1882 to wealthy parents, he was an only child. He went to an expensive private school and then on to Harvard University (the American equivalent to Oxford or Cambridge).

Roosevelt worked as a lawyer before entering politics as a Senator. After only three years he was made Assistant Secretary to the Navy – an important job when America joined the First World War.

At the age of 39 Roosevelt was stricken by polio. Despite his determined efforts, he never regained the proper use of his legs and had to use a wheelchair for much of his life.

Roosevelt never lost his determination to succeed and he re-entered politics in 1928, becoming Governor of New York State. Roosevelt believed that governments should help the poorer citizens. He organised the first scheme by any state to help the unemployed.

Campaign 1932

During the election campaign, Roosevelt did not outline his proposed policies in much detail but he spoke with confidence about what was needed to end the Depression. In particular, he promised:

- government schemes to provide more jobs
- measures to revive industry and agriculture
- relief for the poor and unemployed
- protection for workers against irresponsible employers.

He also won considerable support by promising to get rid of Prohibition, which by now was very unpopular and completely discredited.

Roosevelt was a good public speaker. He also worked hard to take his message to ordinary men and women throughout America. He travelled around the country talking to the people about the problems they faced.

He convinced many voters that: 'Roosevelt is the only president who ever cared for people like us.' Having suffered and overcome fearful blows in his own life, he was well qualified to help the American people overcome theirs.

■ ACTIVITY

Read statements A–F below. They are all from the 1932 presidential election campaign. For each statement decide whether it was made by Roosevelt or Hoover and explain the reasons for your choice.

A

> It is not the function of the government to relieve individuals of their responsibilities to their neighbours.

B

> I pledge you, I pledge myself, to a new deal for the American people.

C

> The country demands bold, persistent experimentation. It is common sense to take a method and try it. If it fails, admit it frankly and try another. But above all, try something.

D

> Prosperity is just around the corner.

E

> When you are told that the President of the United States ... has sat in the White House for the last three years of your misfortune without troubling to know your burden ... without using every ounce of his strength and straining every nerve to protect and help ... then I say to you that such statements are deliberate, intolerable falsehoods [lies].

F

> One of the duties of the state is that of caring for those of its citizens who find themselves the victims of such adverse circumstances as make them unable to obtain even the necessities for mere existence.

■ TASK

Write a campaign speech or an election leaflet for Roosevelt.
  Put in it:

■ the present state of the country
■ the failure of Hoover's government to help people
■ other negative points about the Republican government
■ what you intend to do
■ why your plans will be successful
■ a slogan.

Why did Roosevelt win the election?

Roosevelt won the election with about seven million more votes than Hoover. Hoover won only six states. This was the biggest victory recorded in an American presidential election up to that time.

SOURCE 2 Roosevelt shakes hands with a miner in West Virginia during the 1932 election campaign

SOURCE 1 The Smilette: a Democrat election poster of 1932

SOURCE 3 Frances Perkins, the first woman member of Roosevelt's government after 1933

❝ A newcomer in the national field, Roosevelt had to get out and become known. He saw thousands of Americans . . . He liked going around the country. He used to come back and describe individuals in the crowd – a woman with a baby, an old fellow, small boys scampering in the throng . . . His personal relationship with crowds was on a warm, simple level of friendly, neighbourly exchange of affection. ❞

1. Explain how the poster in Source 1 is attacking Hoover's policies.
2. Look at Source 2.
a) Why is Roosevelt sitting in a car and not standing up shaking hands?
b) What image do you think Roosevelt was trying to create?
c) This picture was taken during the election campaign. Does that make it unreliable as evidence of Roosevelt's attitude to working people? What is it useful evidence of?
3. What reasons do Sources 3 and 4 give for Roosevelt's success?

    Add these to the chart you have already started (see page 95).

SOURCE 4 Roger Smalley, *Depression and the New Deal*

❝ Instead of offering new policies in the election campaign, Hoover concentrated on claiming that things would become far worse if the Democrats gained power . . . this compared badly with the confidence that Roosevelt showed. The Democratic candidate's smile and optimism proved far more popular with the electorate than Hoover's grim looks.

This difference of presentation was important because, in some ways, the two candidates seemed to have similar policies; for example, government support for ailing businesses and job-creation schemes featured in the programmes of both candidates. ❞

I think Mr Roosevelt's got such a nice personality, so cheerful and optimistic. We need someone like that in this Depression ... so unlike that cold Mr Hoover!

Roosevelt got out to meet the people. Look at all the miles he covered during the election. He's been all over the country and people have got to know and like him. People don't like Hoover because he doesn't seem to be interested in their problems.

Yes, Roosevelt certainly seems to care about people. He helped people in trouble in New York State and I think he can do it for the whole country. Any one who can overcome polio must have a strong fighting spirit.

People blame Hoover and the Republicans for the mess and not doing enough about it. They wanted a change. They voted for Roosevelt because they believe he will take real action to deal with the Depression.

I think a good few people voted for Roosevelt because he's promised to end Prohibition. They want a drink – free and legal. They're tired of all the problems Prohibition has caused – the gangsters, the killings, the crooked dealings by big businesses.

■ TASK

Different people had different views about why Roosevelt won the election.

Use your chart and the ideas above to write an essay: Why did Franklin D. Roosevelt win the 1932 Presidential election?

Mention:

■ how people saw Hoover's policies
■ Roosevelt's ideas
■ the way both conducted their campaigns and presented themselves to the public.

"All the News That's Fit to Print."

VOL. LXXXII....No. 27,318.　　Entered as Second-Class Matter, Postoffice, New York, N. Y.　　NEW YOR

ROOSEVELT WINNER IN LANDSLIDE!
DEMOCRATS CONTROL WET CONGRESS;
LEHMAN GOVERNOR, O'BRIEN MAYOR

BIG VOTE FOR M'KEE

O'Brien Is 245,464 Behind Ticket as Protests Rise

BUT FINAL LEAD IS 616,736

Pounds Concedes Defeat Early, Saying 'Day of Miracles Is Past.'

McKEE TOTAL IS 137,538

Thousands of "Write-In" Votes Are Wasted as Backers Fail to Record Choice Properly.

HILLQUIT POLLS 248,425

Gets Greatest Vote in History of City for a Socialist—Runs Far Ahead of Party.

John P. O'Brien, Tam-

THE GOVERNOR-ELECT.

© New York Times Studio.
Colonel Herbert H. Lehman

JUDGES IN 'DEAL' WIN; PROTEST VOTE HEAVY

STATE VICTORY SOLID

Lehman Gets Record Party Plurality of 887,000.

WAGNER CLOSE TO HIM

National Ticket Has Margin of 615,000—Full Slate Is Elected.

RELIEF BONDS ARE VOTED

Republicans Have Narrow Edge Up-State—Hill Admits 'Protest' Defeated Them.

By JAMES A. HAGERTY.

Lieut. Gov. Herbert H. Lehman, Democratic nominee for Governor, defeated Colonel William J. Donovan, Republican, yesterday, in the Democratic whirlwind that swept New York State, by a plurality of about 887,000, a record for a Democratic candidate in this State. Governor Franklin D. Roosevelt

---

The President's Message To the President-Elect

From a Staff Correspondent.
PALO ALTO, Cal., Nov. 8.—President Hoover conceded his defeat for re-election at 9:17 o'clock tonight, Pacific Time, and dispatched this telegram of congratulations to Governor Roosevelt:

Palo Alto, Cal.,
Nov. 8, 1932.
The Hon. Franklin D. Roosevelt, Biltmore Hotel,
New York, N. Y.

I congratulate you on the opportunity that has come to you to be of service to the country and I wish for you a most successful administration. In the common purpose of all of us I shall dedicate myself to every possible helpful effort.

HERBERT HOOVER.

Governor Roosevelt had not received President Hoover's message when he left for his home shortly before 2 o'clock this morning. Pending its receipt he said he preferred not to make any reply or comment on the message.

DEMOCRATS CONTROL STATE SENATE, 26–25

Republican Margin in Assembly of 6 Votes Is Reduced to 2 —Lose by 4 Up-State.

OVERTURN IN SENATE

Bingham, Watson, Moses and Smoot Are Defeated.

DEMOCRATIC MAJORITY 12

Party Adds to Control in House—May Rule Both Branches This Winter.

LA GUARDIA LOSES SEAT

Mrs. Pratt Defeated, Wadsworth Wins—Texas Sends Garner Back to the House.

The Democratic wave of victory yesterday gave that party complete control of Congress and in its onrush carried down to defeat the four Republican leaders of the Senate. Senator Smoot of Utah, Republican dean of the Senate and chairman of the powerful Finance Committee; Senator Watson of Indiana, floor

---

THE PRESIDENT-ELECT.

SWEEP IS NATIONAL

Democrats Carry 40 States, Electoral Votes 448.

SIX STATES FOR HOOVER

He Loses New York, New Jersey, Bay State, Indiana and Ohio.

DEMOCRATS WIN SENATE

Necessary Majority for Repeal of the Volstead Act in Prospect.

RECORD NATIONAL VOTE

Hoover Felicitates Rival and Promises 'Every Helpful Effort for Common Purpose.'

The Hundred Days

ROOSEVELT PROMISED: 'Action, and action now.' But he did not have a clear idea what should be done or how much it would cost. He worked closely with a panel of experts called the BRAIN TRUST to put together a programme of new laws to help America out of the Depression. It was called the New Deal.

The economy was in such a terrible state that Congress realised that drastic measures had to be taken. When Roosevelt demanded extra powers to take action quickly, the Senate and the House of Representatives were prepared to give him the same authority as if the country was being invaded. This special session of Congress lasted exactly 100 days (8 March to 16 June 1933). During this time, thirteen new laws were passed to deal with the emergency.

The New Deal programme had three main aims:

1. Relief
Relieve extreme poverty, feed the starving and stop people losing their homes or farms.

2. Recovery
Revive the economy by getting industry going and people working again.

3. Reform
Make the USA a better place for ordinary people by bringing in measures such as unemployment insurance and old-age pensions, and help for the sick, disabled and needy.

SOURCE 1 Franklin D. Roosevelt, inaugural speech, March 1933

" This is pre-eminently the time to speak the truth, the whole truth, frankly and boldly. Nor need we shrink from honestly facing conditions in our country today. This great nation will endure as it has endured, will revive and will prosper.

So first of all let me assert my firm belief that the only thing we have to fear is fear itself – nameless, unreasoning, unjustified terror which paralyses needed efforts to convert retreat into advance . . .

Our greatest primary task is to put people to work. This is no unsolvable problem if we face it wisely and courageously. "

SOURCE 2 Hugh Brogan, *History of the United States of America*, 1985

" [The inaugural speech] was one of the turning points of American history. In a few minutes Roosevelt did what had so wearyingly eluded Hoover for four years: he gave back to his countrymen their hope and their energy. By the end of the week half a million grateful letters had poured into the White House. "

SOURCE 3 A cartoon about Roosevelt's New Deal, March 1933

1. How could Roosevelt justify the powers he asked Congress to give him?
2. Look at Source 3.
a) Who is putting out the dustbin?
b) Who is walking away?
c) What does the dustbin contain and how are these connected to the man walking away?
d) What is the message of this cartoon?
e) Do you think this reflected the views of many Americans in 1933?
3. How do Sources 1, 2 and 3 show that Roosevelt's government was different from Hoover's?

Talking to the people

Roosevelt realised how important it was to gain the trust of the American people and inspire their confidence. So, just eight days after his inauguration, he gave the first of his famous radio broadcasts which became known as 'fireside chats'. He explained his actions in a simple and direct way, and asked Americans to work with him. Roosevelt's broadcasts were astonishingly successful, none more so than the first one, which dealt with the important issue of the banks.

Sorting out the banks

When Roosevelt became President his most urgent problem was to rescue the banks.

Since 1930, over 5000 banks had been forced to close and the banking system was on the point of collapse. This is because savers had withdrawn their money and businesses had been unable to repay bank loans.

Roosevelt immediately closed all the banks for a 'four-day holiday' and rushed an Emergency Banking Act through Congress in just eight hours. Only the banks that the government decided were honest and well run were allowed to reopen. These banks were supported by government loans to help them to continue operating and to reassure people that their money would be safe. The public's confidence in the banking system was restored and customers redeposited $1 billion shortly after the banks reopened.

SOURCE 4 Roosevelt addressing the American people by radio

Ending Prohibition

Roosevelt brought Prohibition to an end in 1933. Breweries were legalised again and Americans could enjoy a drink without fear of arrest. This made many Americans a lot more cheerful.

SOURCE 6 A crowd in New York celebrates with alcohol, just one minute after the end of Prohibition

SOURCE 5 Interview given by Raymond Moley, a member of the *Brain Trust,* in the 1960s

❝ When people were able to survive the shock of having all the banks closed, and then see the banks open up, with their money protected, there began to be confidence. Good times were coming. ❞

4. Why was it so important to establish public confidence in the banks?
5. Why do you think the 'fireside chats' were a good idea?
6. What do you think would be the main benefits of ending Prohibition?

The alphabet agencies

UNLIKE HOOVER, ROOSEVELT was prepared to provide a huge amount of government money for relief of the needy.

During the 'Hundred Days' in 1933, Roosevelt set up the first of a series of government agencies designed to give the American people much needed help and support. They quickly became known by their initials and so were called the 'alphabet agencies'.

Helping the farmers

The **Farm Credit Administration (FCA)** made loans to a fifth of all farmers so that they would not lose their farms.

The **Agricultural Adjustment Agency (AAA)** paid farmers to produce less food, by taking land out of production or reducing their livestock. Less produce meant the prices went up, and between 1933 and 1939 farmers' incomes doubled. Cotton farmers were paid to plough up ten million acres already planted. The government bought and killed six million piglets in 1933. Some of the meat was tinned and given to the poor, but about nine-tenths was destroyed.

The AAA helped the farmers but not the tenants and sharecroppers who worked on the land. Many of them were evicted because there was not so much work for them to do and farmers replaced them with machinery which they bought with government money.

1. There was a public outcry against the AAA's policies of killing pigs and ploughing up cotton-growing land when so many people were hungry and in need of clothes.
   a) How could Roosevelt and his advisers justify this?
   b) Why didn't they just give away an enormous amount of free food to starving Americans?

Work for the unemployed

The **Civilian Conservation Corps (CCC)** gave jobs to single men under 25. They lived in government camps in the countryside and did hard work such as clearing land, planting trees to stop soil blowing away, and strengthening river banks for flood control. The young men got food and clothing (and a sense of purpose) and most of their small wages ($1 a day) were sent home to help their parents. It was also hoped that the men, who came mainly from the cities, would become fit and healthy as a result of the fresh air.

Between 1933 and 1942 nearly three million men took part in the CCC scheme. Some people criticised it as cheap labour but it was not compulsory, and those who did join learnt skills that could help them get jobs afterwards. Roosevelt later said that he thought the CCC was one of the best achievements of the New Deal.

The **Civilian Works Administration** (CWA) was designed as a short-term scheme to give as many people jobs as possible (four million over the winter of 1933–34). Some useful work, such as building roads, was carried out, but many of the jobs, such as sweeping up leaves in parks or getting out-of-work actors to give free shows, simply gave people something to do.

The aim of the **Public Works Administration (PWA)**, on the other hand, was to create public works of real and lasting value. $7 billion was spent employing skilled men to build dams, bridges, sewage systems and houses. Between 1933 and 1939, the PWA built 70 per cent of America's schools and 35 per cent of America's hospitals.

Helping the needy

The **Federal Emergency Relief Administration (FERA)** was given $500 million to help thousands of Americans who were homeless, penniless and on the brink of starvation. Most of the money was used to increase the number of soup kitchens and to provide clothing, schools and employment schemes.

The **Home Owners Loan Corporation (HOLC)** loaned money to over a million people to prevent them from losing their homes.

Getting industry on its feet

The **National Recovery Administration (NRA)** was set up by the National Industrial Recovery Act (NIRA). The aims of the NRA were:

■ to increase workers' wages so that they would have more money to spend on goods.
■ to increase the prices of factory goods (which had dropped to rock bottom) to help the factory owners make more profit and employ more men.
■ to give workers a fairer deal in the workplace, including better working conditions and shorter hours.

Codes were drawn up for each industry which owners and businessmen were encouraged to sign. These codes fixed prices for the goods, limited workers' hours, set minimum wages and forbade child labour. Workers were given the right to join trade unions and brutal strike-breaking practices were outlawed.

Businesses that signed up were allowed to use the NRA's sign – the Blue Eagle. Big publicity campaigns and parades encouraged the public to buy goods from members of the scheme.

SOURCE 1 'The Spirit of the New Deal', an American cartoon from 1933

2. a) Why do you think the CCC was condemned as a cheap labour plan?
   b) What were its benefits?
3. Why was so much money pumped into public work schemes in the CWA and PWA?
4. a) Who do the people in Source 1 represent?
   b) How does the cartoon explain how the NRA was supposed to work?

The TVA

The Tennessee Valley Authority (TVA) was set up to develop the Tennessee Valley, a vast area which cut through seven states. It was a poverty-stricken area with soil erosion and flooding. The TVA organised the building of 33 dams to control the Tennessee River. Measures were taken to improve the quality of the soil so that it could be farmed again, and new forests were planted. A new 650-mile waterway linking major river systems gave easy access to the area.

Power stations were built at the dams to provide cheap electricity for farmers and domestic consumers. In fact, the TVA became the biggest producer of electricity in America. Industries, such as light engineering, moved into the area to take advantage of cheap power.

The TVA was one of the most impressive schemes of the New Deal, combining an attempt to revive agriculture and industry in one programme.

Thousands of jobs were created, the land was conserved and improved, and health and welfare facilities were provided. Local inhabitants were asked to help plan the scheme. It gave an entire region a chance to recover from the worst effects of the Depression.

5. Why was the development of the Tennessee Valley so impressive?
6. Why might some critics attack this project (clue: American free enterprise)?
7. Some Americans complained that the New Deal schemes, especially the TVA, interfered with the free market in America.
a) What did they mean by the free market?
b) Give three examples of how the New Deal schemes interfered with it.

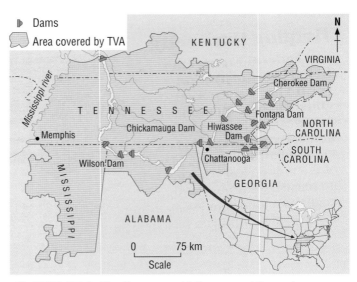

SOURCE 2 The Tennessee Valley passed through seven states with over two million inhabitants, covering 80,000 square miles

SOURCE 3 The Norris Dam, built by the TVA between 1933 and 1936

■ TASK

Draw a chart like the one below. Decide whether an agency was concerned with relief, recovery or reform and put a tick in the appropriate column(s). (Remember that some agencies served more than one purpose.) In the final column explain why. One example has been completed for you.

Agency	Relief	Recovery	Reform	Explanation
CCC	√			Gave young men jobs, food and a small wage. Relief from unemployment in the cities, and the chance to become fit and healthy

How was the Second New Deal different from the First?

MOST OF THE alphabet agencies were set up by 1935 but there was still work to be done and further important measures were introduced between 1935 and 1937. On the whole, these were aimed at reforming aspects of American society and improving conditions for ordinary people. They have been called the Second New Deal.

The Works Progress Administration (WPA), 1935

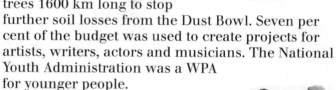

The WPA gave work to about two million people a year. They built roads, public buildings, schools, bridges, tunnels, sewers, and a windbreak of trees 1600 km long to stop further soil losses from the Dust Bowl. Seven per cent of the budget was used to create projects for artists, writers, actors and musicians. The National Youth Administration was a WPA for younger people.

The Social Security Act, 1935

By the 1930s many European countries had introduced some form of social security to help the old, the sick and the unemployed. Americans had believed that individuals should provide for their own future. In 1935 Roosevelt introduced the Social Security Act, which proposed to give a state pension to everyone over 65, and to support handicapped people, and mothers with dependent children. It also proposed an unemployment insurance scheme to be provided by the individual states, with aid from the federal government.

The Wagner Act, 1935

In 1935 Senator Robert Wagner introduced an Act to support workers who wanted to form a union and to prevent employers from sacking workers who were union members. Trade unions gradually began to gain more power and employers had to listen to them.

The Resettlement Administration, 1935; and the Farm Security Administration, 1937

The AAA of 1933 had helped farm owners but it had not helped sharecroppers, tenants or farm workers. Indeed, many of them were evicted as land was taken out of production. In 1935 Roosevelt set up the Resettlement Administration (RA) to help these groups. It aimed to move 500,000 families to better land and to resettle them in new houses.

In 1937 the RA was replaced by the Farm Security Administration (FSA), which gave loans to sharecroppers and tenant farmers to buy their own land. The FSA also set up labour camps which helped migrant farm workers to live in better conditions. Despite this help, the plight of poor farm workers remained grim in the 1930s.

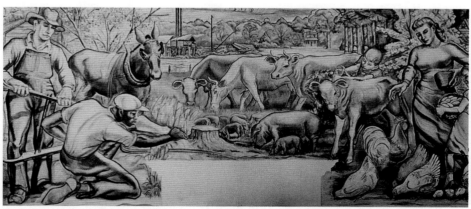

SOURCE 1 *Spring* by Caroline S. Rohland, painted for Sylvania, Georgia. Thousands of artists were funded by the WPA. They worked on paintings and exhibited their work. They also painted murals on public buildings and made sculptures for public places. These transformed the appearance of some areas in the cities

1. a) Add the measures of the Second New Deal to the chart you drew for the First New Deal (see page 104).
    b) In what ways are they similar to, and in what ways different from, the measures of the (first) Hundred Days?
2. What do you think the Second New Deal was trying to achieve?

■ REVIEW ACTIVITY

Study Sources 1–7 below. Link each source to the work of one of the alphabet agencies described on pages 102–105, fully explaining the reasons for your choice.

S OURCE 1

S OURCE 2

SOURCE 3 From *New Deal and War* by W.E. Leuchtenburg, 1964

❝ The _____ program left much to be desired. People on direct relief felt humiliated. Applying for assistance was like making a formal admission of inadequacy. The applicant's esteem suffered another blow when an investigator entered his home to ascertain whether his application was truthful. Relief recipients were often too proud to go to the depot to accept surplus commodities lest they be recognised. ❞

SOURCE 4 Cotton being ploughed back into the land

SOURCE 5

SOURCE 6

SOURCE 7

Why did Roosevelt win the biggest ever landslide victory in the presidential election of 1936?

IN 1936 ROOSEVELT faced his second presidential election. It gave the voters their chance to show what they thought about Roosevelt and the New Deal.

The Republican Party chose Alfred Landon, a respected and popular politician, as their candidate. They tried to use criticism of the President and his policies to win back the support they had lost in 1932. But Roosevelt won again, with over 27 million votes, the most that any President has received in American history. He won a majority in all but two states. The people had made clear what they thought.

SOURCE 1 From a New Jersey factory notice board, 1933

66 President Roosevelt has done his part; now you do something. Buy something – buy anything, paint your kitchen, send a telegram, give a party, get a car, pay a bill, rent a flat, fix your roof, get a haircut, see a show, build a house, take a trip, sing a song, get married.

It does not matter what you do – but get going and keep going. This old world is starting to move. 99

SOURCE 2 Thousands of personal letters were written to Roosevelt. This is one of them

66 Dear Mr President,
This is just to tell you everything is alright now. The man you sent found our house alright and we went down to the bank with him and the mortgage can go on for a while longer. You remember I wrote about losing the furniture too. Well, your man got it back for us. I never heard of a President like you, Mr Roosevelt. Mrs _____ and I are old folks, and don't amount to much, but we are joined with millions of others in praying for you every night. God bless you, Mr Roosevelt. 99

SOURCE 3 'Yes, you remembered me.' A cartoon from 1933

SOURCE 4 Hugh Brogan, 'The New Deal', *Purnell's History of the 20th Century*

66 In his 'fireside chats' on the radio he projected himself and his message into millions of homes. Most years until the war, he made extensive tours through America so that hundreds of thousands saw for themselves the big smile, the jauntily-cocked cigarette-holder, the pince-nez, straight nose and jutting jaw made familiar by photographs and cartoons. 99

SOURCE 5 Justice William O. Douglas, *Being an American*, 1948

66 *He was in a very special sense the people's President, because he made them feel that with him in the White House they shared the Presidency. The sense of sharing the Presidency gave even the most humble citizen a lively sense of belonging.* 99

SOURCE 7 W.E. Leuchtenburg, *Franklin D. Roosevelt and the New Deal*, 1963

66 *Negroes swung to Roosevelt because they had been granted relief. In many areas, Negroes, hit harder than any other group by the depression, survived largely because of relief cheques ... The NYA, through the noted negro leader, Mary McLeod Bethume, funnelled funds to thousands of young Negroes ...*

... When Roosevelt toured the country in 1936, thousands of men and women pressed up to railroad tracks for a glimpse of the President. There was something terrible about their response, he told Ickes. He could hear people crying out: 'He saved my home,' 'He gave me a job.' 99

SOURCE 6 Frances Perkins, Labour Secretary in Roosevelt's cabinet, *The Roosevelt I Knew*, 1947

66 *As Roosevelt described it, the 'New Deal' meant that the forgotten man, the little man, the man nobody knew much about, was going to be dealt better cards to play with ... He understood that the suffering of the Depression had fallen with terrific impact upon the people least able to bear it. He knew that the rich had been hit hard too, but at least they had something left. But the little merchant, the small householder and home owner, the farmer, the man who worked for himself – these people were desperate. And Roosevelt saw them as principal citizens of the United States, numerically and in their importance to the maintenance of the ideals of American democracy.* 99

1. Use Sources 1–7 to work out why Roosevelt was so popular and received such an enormous personal vote. You could use a chart like the one below:

Source	What it tells us	How this helped Roosevelt in the election

2. a) Why is Frances Perkins in Source 6:

   ■ a good source on Roosevelt
   ■ a source whose opinions you have to treat with some care?

   b) Which other sources here support her opinion?

3. In the 1936 elections, support for Roosevelt came from farmers, the unemployed, black people and trade unionists. Use what you have learned in this section on the New Deal (pages 102–109) to explain why this was the case.

Who did not support the New Deal?

Opposition from those who believed the New Deal interfered too much in people's lives

The result of the 1936 election showed that the majority of people supported Roosevelt. However, many Americans remained opposed to the New Deal throughout the 1930s. Over sixteen million voted for the Republican Party in the election. This is no surprise – America was a country which had been built on the ideas of individual effort and SELF-RELIANCE, with minimum government intervention in the lives of the people.

SOURCE 1 A cartoon entitled 'Priming the Pump', published in an American newspaper in 1933.

Republicans

The Republicans claimed that Roosevelt was behaving like a dictator and making the government too powerful. He was even compared to Hitler and Stalin. They said that the TVA and NRA schemes were just like the communist ECONOMIC PLANNING of the Soviet Union. They believed that the Social Security Act would undermine the American way of life by making people lazy and dependent on government help.

The Republicans also objected to the huge cost of the New Deal. They claimed that much of the money was being wasted; for example, the WPA was paying people to do unnecessary jobs.

Business

Business leaders did not like government interference in their affairs. They were angry about Roosevelt's support for trade unions and the campaign to raise wages. They disliked having to pay social security contributions for their workers. They objected to schemes like the TVA, which they said competed unfairly with privately owned businesses. They criticised all the codes and regulations of the NRA and other agencies as confusing and difficult to administer.

In 1934 a group of business leaders formed the Liberty League to oppose the New Deal.

SOURCE 2 Cartoon from the *Philadelphia Enquirer*

1. Draw up a list of ways some people thought the New Deal interfered too much in their lives.
2. Why do you think the opposition to the New Deal was so strong?

S OURCE 3 A cartoon from the 1930s, commenting on President Roosevelt's actions

SOURCE 4 From an article, 'They Hate Roosevelt', *Harpers*, May 1936

66 A resident of Park Avenue [area where the rich lived] in New York City was sentenced not long ago to a term of imprisonment for threatening violence to the person of President Roosevelt. This episode ... was significant as a dramatically extreme manifestation of the fanatical hatred of the President which today obsesses thousands of men and women among the American upper class. 99

The rich

Many wealthy Americans resented having to pay higher taxes to pay for the work of the New Deal agencies. They were bitter that Roosevelt's policies had taken away some of their power.

S OURCE 5 A cartoon from the 1930s. The caption for this cartoon read, 'Mother, Wilfred wrote a bad word'

3. What are Sources 1 and 2 saying is wrong with the New Deal?
4. What view of Roosevelt is the cartoon in Source 3 supporting?
    Explain your answer, referring to the cartoon.
5. a) How does Source 4 help explain the message of the cartoon in Source 5? What are they both saying?
    b) How reliable is the opinion in Source 4?
6. a) In what ways are the cartoons in Sources 1, 3 and 5 useful as historical evidence?
    b) What are the problems of using cartoons as evidence?

■ **TASK**

Write a letter from a rich Republican business leader to a newspaper, attacking Roosevelt and the New Deal.

Opposition from those who believed the New Deal was not doing enough

In 1936 there were still around nine million unemployed in the USA. Although this was a reduction of over four million since Roosevelt became President in 1932, it was seen as failure by critics who wanted the government to take even more RADICAL action. Some groups who had been badly affected by the Depression had still not received any help by 1936. For example, the old did not receive pensions until 1940 and the plight of many agricultural workers remained desperate, despite the work of the Resettlement Administration. Three of Roosevelt's main critics were Huey Long, Doctor Townsend and Father Coughlin.

Huey 'Kingfish' Long

Huey Long had been elected Governor of Louisiana, a poor southern state, in 1928. He had won the election by promising to increase taxes for the rich and use the money to build more roads, hospitals and schools. Once in office, he carried out his promises but he used bribery and corruption to run the state.

At first Long supported the New Deal but by 1934 he was attacking it for not doing enough for the poor. He proposed a 'Share our Wealth' scheme. He wanted all personal fortunes of over $5 million to be confiscated and the money shared out. He said every American family should be given between $4000 and $5000. He also promised a minimum wage, houses for war veterans, pensions and completely free education.

Long remained popular with whites in Louisiana and had a following across the USA. But he also had many opponents and in 1935 he was assassinated by a young doctor.

Doctor Francis Townsend

Doctor Townsend had one very specific idea. He proposed that everyone over the age of 60 should get a pension of $200 a month provided they spent the money during the month and gave up their jobs. He thought this would provide jobs for young people, create a demand for goods, and help the old who had been neglected. Many older people liked his idea and 7000 'Townsend Clubs' sprang up across the USA.

Father Coughlin, the 'radio priest'

Father Coughlin broadcast his ideas on radio to some 40 million Americans on Sunday evenings during 'the Golden Hour of the Little Flower'. (St Therese, the Little Flower of Jesus, near Detroit, was his church.) His praise for Roosevelt at the beginning of the New Deal soon turned to vicious attacks. He accused Roosevelt of failing to tackle the problems of the poor. He set up the National Union for Social Justice which attracted millions of members from all over America.

However, his ideas were rather confused and his audience had largely faded away by 1940.

7. a) Why do you think the ideas of Long and Townsend were attractive to many Americans?
   b) Why did they not have much chance of being put into action?
8. What did this opposition reveal about the failings of the New Deal?

■ ACTIVITY

Look at statements A–F below, which all criticise the New Deal. Match
each statement to the person you think would have said it.

■ rich, upper-class woman
■ businessman
■ Republican politician
■ Huey Long follower
■ member of a Townsend club
■ Father Coughlin listener

A

> Nothing has been done for the old people
> and millions of young people are still out of
> work. I'd gladly give up my job to help
> someone younger if the state guaranteed
> that I had enough to live on in my old age.

B

> I'm sick of the government
> taking all my money in taxes and
> spending it on people who are
> too lazy to make their own way
> in the world.

C

> Is this America or the Soviet Union?
> Look at the Tennessee Valley! This is
> socialist economic planning, not
> American free enterprise. The
> government is getting involved in
> everything. It is interfering in people's
> lives and wasting billions of dollars.
> We're destroying the values this
> country was built on.

D

> Roosevelt is not doing enough to
> help the people suffering most. It's
> time that they were treated more
> fairly. There are farm workers
> living in terrible poverty, and
> workers in this city who barely
> earn enough to feed their families.
> The American people are getting a
> raw deal not a New Deal.

F

> It's time we dealt with the money-
> grabbing rich. They will never
> give up their money willingly. We
> should force them to hand it over
> to pay for schools, pensions and
> hospitals. All American families
> should have a house and a car. If
> everybody earned a fair wage,
> they would be able to spend
> money on goods and that would
> mean enough jobs for everyone.

E

> The New Deal helped us in the beginning
> but now it is causing problems. There are so
> many rules and regulations that it is
> becoming difficult to run a business. And the
> government is encouraging the trade unions
> to ask for higher wages and shorter hours:
> already we are seeing strikes and disruption.
> Profits are falling and businesses will
> collapse.

The Supreme Court and the New Deal

THE SUPREME COURT of the USA is a very powerful body. It can block any measures by the President and any laws passed by Congress if the judges decide that these are unconstitutional (not allowed by the Constitution). The judges of the Supreme Court in the 1930s were mainly Republicans. They believed that the New Deal was undermining the American Constitution, which was designed to defend individual freedom against excessive government control.

Supreme Court judgments

In 1935 the Supreme Court ruled that the National Industrial Recovery Act (NIRA) was unconstitutional because the Constitution did not allow a President to make laws to control businesses.

In 1936, it declared that measures taken by the Agricultural Adjustment Administration were unconstitutional on the grounds that regulations about agriculture could only be made by individual states and not by central government.

Several other New Deal measures were also attacked by the Supreme Court judges.

Roosevelt's response to the Supreme Court

Roosevelt was determined that the Supreme Court should not stop his reforms. The nine judges of the Supreme Court were all old, and six of them were over 70. Roosevelt wanted them to retire but he could not force them to do so. Following his sweeping victory in the 1936 presidential election, he asked Congress to give him the power to appoint six new judges to the Court.

He would be able to pick judges who he knew would be sympathetic to the New Deal. However, Roosevelt's attempt to 'pack the court' with judges who agreed with him caused alarm across America, even amongst his own supporters. Many Democrats thought that this would give the President too much power. Some accused him of wanting to rule America as a dictator. There was overwhelming opposition from Congress and Roosevelt's plan was rejected.

Nevertheless the judges had been shaken by the President's action and some of them retired voluntarily soon afterwards. The new judges were less hostile to the New Deal. Most of the useful parts of the NIRA were accepted by the Court in more carefully constructed laws. When the Wagner Act and the Social Security Act were reviewed by the Court later in 1937, they were both judged to be constitutional, despite their unpopularity with many Republicans.

> ### The 'Sick Chicken' Case
> The Schechter Poultry Corporation, which had signed up to the NRA codes on fair trading, had been accused of breaking NIRA codes on several occasions. One of the offences was the sale of an 'unfit chicken' to a butcher. The dispute went to court. The Schechter Corporation was found guilty of breaking the codes. But it appealed against the verdict. The appeal was heard by the Supreme Court. The Supreme Court ruled that the President's agencies could not interfere in matters of trade inside a state. The Schechter Corporation was acquitted and the NRA code was declared illegal. The so-called 'Sick Chicken' Case contributed to the NRA being declared unconstitutional.

1. Write brief notes explaining the argument between the Supreme Court and Roosevelt over the New Deal measures.
2. a) Why were a large number of Americans alarmed by Roosevelt's plan to appoint his supporters as Supreme Court judges?
   b) Why did Congress oppose him?

SOURCE 1   A cartoon from the *Chicago Tribune*, September 1935

THE ILLEGAL ACT.

PRESIDENT ROOSEVELT. "I'M SORRY, BUT THE SUPREME COURT SAYS I MUST CHUCK YOU BACK AGAIN."

SOURCE 3   *Punch* cartoon, June 1935. The President is saying 'I'm sorry, but the Supreme Court says I must chuck you back again.'

SOURCE 2   A cartoon showing Roosevelt lassoing a Supreme Court judge

3. Look carefully at Source 1.
a) What is a 'Trojan horse'?
b) Where is the Trojan horse about to be taken?
c) What is the cartoonist saying?
4. What is the message of Source 2?
5. The British cartoon (Source 3) from *Punch* presents a different view of the struggle between Roosevelt and the Supreme Court.
a) Explain what the message of the cartoon is.
b) Do you think many Americans would have agreed with this cartoon?

HOW SUCCESSFUL WAS THE NEW DEAL?

AFTER THE STRUGGLE with the Supreme Court, the New Deal appeared to be running out of steam, especially when a second wave of depression hit America in 1937–38. The reforming days were largely over and in January 1939 Roosevelt acknowledged that the New Deal had come to an end.

The New Deal was a complex series of measures requiring a huge number of laws to be passed by Congress. We have only mentioned the most important ones here. Historians agree that the New Deal had a major impact on America, but they argue about how successful it was. They put the following key questions about the New Deal:

- Did the New Deal reforms make life better for all Americans?
- Did the New Deal bring economic recovery?
- How effective were the measures designed to bring relief and recovery – did they work?

Overview: what did the New Deal achieve?

THE MAIN AIMS of the New Deal were the recovery of industry and agriculture, and to get people back to work. Did it succeed?

There is no doubt that the first phase of the New Deal from 1933 to 1936 brought about a degree of recovery. Unemployment was reduced and businesses were revived. But when, in 1937, the government started to spend less money on its schemes, production fell again and a second wave of depression hit the country.

Roosevelt pumped billions of dollars into the economy to prevent the situation getting worse. However, it was clear that continual injections of government money were needed. It was only after 1941, when the USA became involved in the Second World War and the demand for American manufactured goods and food increased dramatically, that the economy was lifted out of depression.

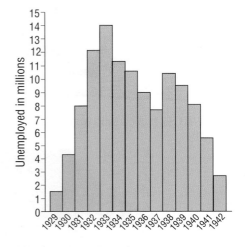

SOURCE 1 Unemployment in the USA 1929–45

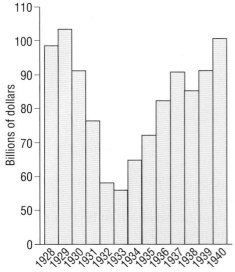

SOURCE 2 America's Gross National Product (GNP). The GNP is a measure of how much a country produces

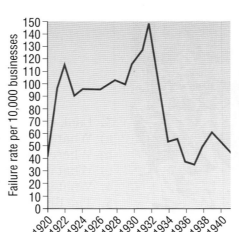
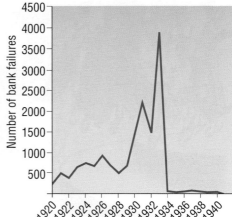

SOURCE 3 The number of business and bank failures in the USA 1920–41

1. Look at Source 1.

a) Use the figures to describe the pattern of unemployment from 1931 to 1936.

b) In 1938 the government spent less money. What happened to unemployment? (See Source 1.)

c) How many people were still out of work in 1939?

d) In what year did the figures drop significantly?

2. Do the production figures in Source 2 tell the same or a different story? Explain your answer, referring to the figures in different years.

3. What does Source 3 tell us about the success of the New Deal?

4. Taking the evidence of the graphs and Sources 1 and 4:

■ did the New Deal bring recovery up to 1939?

■ what finally brought the total of jobless down and raised the level of production?

Refer to the evidence from the sources in your answers.

SOURCE 4 W.E. Leuchtenburg, *Franklin D. Roosevelt and the New Deal*, 1963

66 *The New Deal never demonstrated that it could achieve prosperity in peacetime ... As late as 1941 there were still six million unemployed and not until the war did the army of jobless finally disappear.* 99

SOURCE 5 Sean Dennis Cashman, *America in the Twenties and Thirties*

66 *The New Deal ... left largely untouched the problems of tenant farmers, sharecroppers, migrant workers in agriculture and, among ethnic groups, blacks, Puerto Ricans, and Mexican-Americans ...*

It bypassed black Americans, made only symbolic concessions to the status of women, and did little to improve the general standard of education. 99

SOURCE 6 'The New Deal in Review 1936–1940', in *New Republic*, 20 May 1940

66 *The New Deal has clearly done far more for the general welfare of the country and its citizens than any administration in the previous history of the nation. Its relief for the underprivileged in city and country has been indispensable. Without this relief an appalling amount of misery would have resulted ... In addition, the New Deal has accomplished much of permanent benefit to the nation.* 99

SOURCE 7 C.P. Hill, *Franklin Roosevelt*, 1966

66 *What did the New Deal achieve ... It certainly did not cure the Depression. And many economists have maintained that on balance it did not even do much to help American business to recover ...*

Yet, it had notable positive achievements to its credit. The transformation of the Tennessee Valley under the TVA from much poverty to a growing measure of prosperity was one. The PWA [Public Works Administration] ... built on a considerable scale – schools and sewage plants, hospitals, railway stations, bridges etc ... the WPA [Works Progress Administration] also gave work to writers, painters, sculptors and actors. But far more significant was the simple fact that the New Deal restored hope to millions of men and women, by providing them with a job or saving their home. 99

5. Look back at pages 102–105. Find three groups of Americans that the New Deal helped and explain how it helped them?

6. Which groups, according to Source 5, did it not help? You can find out more about some of these groups on pages 118–119.

7. What particular help did it give to millions of people and why was this so important. Source 6 will help you.

8. a) What other achievements does Christopher Hill (Source 7) credit to the New Deal?

b) Can you add any others from your own study of pages 101–105?

Did the New Deal reforms make life better for all Americans?

Did they do enough for black people?

Blacks remained second-class citizens. There was still widespread racism and discrimination. In the South, segregation continued in education, transport and in public places. This was continued in the New Deal: blacks were put in segregated CCC camps, and when the new town of Norris was built in the Tennessee Valley, blacks were not allowed to live there. Black people found it hard to get work. By 1935, around 30 per cent were living on relief. Jobs were usually given to whites and the jobs that blacks did get were often menial ones. The 1940 census showed that only one in twenty blacks had a desk job compared with one in three whites.

Roosevelt failed to put through civil rights laws, particularly an anti-lynching law. He claimed he needed the support of the Democratic congressmen in the South to carry through the New Deal, and they were firmly opposed to civil rights for blacks or any measures to help them as a special group.

Although black people did not benefit from the New Deal as much as whites, thousands did receive much more relief than ever before. Around 200,000 blacks benefited from the CCC programme and they got a large share of housing in slum-clearance projects. Also, black people were given positions of responsibility in the New Deal administration.

SOURCE 2 W.L. Katz, *Eyewitness: the Negro in American History*, 1967, talking about his experience in the Civilian Conservation Corps

66 *I went Monday morning at 8 o'clock to Pier 1, North river. There were, I suppose, more than 1,000 boys standing about the pier ... The coloured boys were a goodly sprinkling of the whole ...*

[The boys were taken to a camp in New Jersey]

Before we left the bus the officer shouted emphatically: 'Coloured boys fall out in the rear.' The coloured from several buses were herded together, and stood in line until after the white boys had been registered and taken to their tents ...

We [blacks] were taken to a permanent camp in the Upper South. This camp was a dream compared with Camp Dix. There was plenty to eat, and we slept in barracks instead of tents ... At the 'rec' [recreation hall] we had a radio, a piano, a store called a 'canteen', ... a baseball team, boxing squad ... and classes in various arts and crafts ... During the first week, we did no work outside the camp, but only hiked, drilled and exercised. [We] worked five days a week, eight hours a day. Our bosses were local men, Southerners, but on the whole, I found nothing to complain of. The work varied, but it was always healthy, outdoor labour ... 99

SOURCE 1 Black people queuing for relief, 1937

1. a) Do you think the photograph in Source 1 was posed or did the photographer just happen to see the queue in front of this poster?
   b) How reliable is this photograph?
   c) Why do you think the photograph was taken and published?
2. What evidence is there in Sources 1 and 2 that blacks still faced discrimination in the New Deal?
3. What was Roosevelt's justification for not helping black people more in the southern states?
4. To what extent did American blacks gain from the New Deal?

Did they help native American Indians?

A number of New Deal measures were aimed directly at improving the situation of native American Indians.

The Indian Re-organisation Act of 1934 provided money to buy reservation land so that it could be owned by tribes rather than individuals (this would stop outsiders taking over). Government loans helped native American Indians to set up businesses and buy farming equipment. The amount of land they owned went up from 47 million acres to 50 million acres.

The Indian Reservation Act of 1934 gave native American Indians the right to manage their own affairs, such as setting up their own courts of law. They were encouraged to follow their own cultural and religious traditions.

Did they do much for women?

Few of the New Deal measures were aimed at women. Many of the programmes were based around construction and manual labour, traditionally the work of men. Only about 8000 women were included in the CCC programme. The number of women employed did go up during the 1930s, but this was largely because they were cheap labour. Their average wage was half that of men in 1937.

The Social Security Act required the state governments to provide money for women and their dependent children. But a number of states tried to avoid paying this by introducing other conditions such as no payments for women with illegitimate children.

One area where women did advance was in the New Deal agencies themselves. Women were given positions of responsibility, running the agencies. Mary Macleod Bethume, a black woman, became head of the National Youth Administration and helped thousands of young blacks. The biggest success story was that of Francis Perkins who became Secretary of Labour in Roosevelt's government. This was the first time a woman had reached such a high level. Perkins was responsible for supervising many of the New Deal Labour regulations.

SOURCE 3 Hugh Brogan, *History of the United States of America*

   66 *By the time the enemies of the red man won national power again, after the Second World War, the Indians had recovered so far that they were able to beat off the attackers and begin the slow rise which, with many setbacks, has characterised their history ever since. This was one of the most complete and heart-warming successes of the New Deal.* 99

SOURCE 4 Francis Perkins, Secretary of Labour, 1933–45

5. Why does Hugh Brogan in Source 3 think that the New Deal was very successful for native American Indians?
6. Why do you think there were few direct measures to improve the position of women in the workforce?

Did the New Deal help labour unions?

LABOUR UNREST grew in the early 1930s. Unemployed workers staged demonstrations that were often met with violence, as in 1930 when police attacked a crowd of 35,000 demonstrators in New York.

It was clear that labour unions could not achieve anything without government support. The National Recovery Agency (NRA) gave workers the right to bargain collectively. However, as membership of the NRA's schemes was voluntary employers could ignore them. The Wagner Act of 1935 gave labour unions greater protection and workers more rights, yet many employers still refused to recognise them.

As far as the workers were concerned, they had government support in their struggle. There was a wave of violent industrial conflicts in the mid-1930s. In 1934 in Toledo, Ohio, a seven-hour battle took place between strikers and National Guardsmen. In 1935 several unions joined together to form the Committee for Industrial Organisation (CIO) which was big enough to bargain with the giant companies. They organised strikes and sit-ins.

One of the main targets of the CIO was the steel industry. Some of the steel companies gave in and signed contracts recognising unions and agreeing basic hours and wages. But other companies decided to bring in strike-breaking armies. In Chicago this led to the 'Memorial Day Massacre' in 1937. The Republic Steel Company refused to negotiate a contract, so the CIO organised a strike of its workers. On 31 May strikers and their families marching outside the factory were attacked by 500 armed Chicago police. Ten marchers were killed and 90 wounded.

SOURCE 2 B. Stolberg, *The Story of the CIO*, 1938, describing how the Ford Motor Company went to great lengths to stop its workers forming unions

66 *There are about eight hundred underworld characters in the Ford Service organization. They are the Storm Troops. They make no pretence of working, but are merely 'keeping order' in the plant community through terror ... There are between 8000 and 9000 authentic workers, a great many of them spies and stool-pigeons and a great many others who have been browbeaten into joining this industrial mafia ... Workers seen talking together are taken off the assembly line and fired. Every man suspected of union sympathies is immediately discharged, usually under the framed-up charge of 'starting a fight', in which he often gets terribly beaten up.* 99

SOURCE 1 B. Stolberg, *The Story of the CIO*, 1938

66 *Many companies acquired impressive arsenals of weapons to 'protect their property' and break strikes. In 1937, half of all tear gas and the equipment needed to use it was bought by industrial companies. In the same year, Youngstown Sheet and Tube Co. [a steel company] possessed the following munitions:*

machine guns	8
rifles	369
shotguns	190
revolvers	454
gas guns	109
rounds of gas ammunition	3000
rounds of ball ammunition	6000
rounds of shot ammunition	3950 99

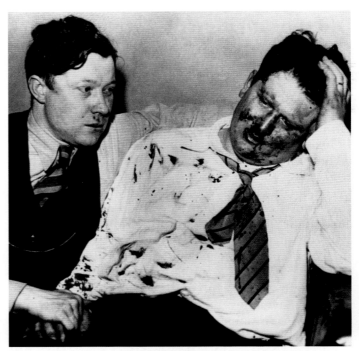

SOURCE 3 A trade union leader who was beaten up by security guards at the Ford factory

Despite setbacks, the struggle paid off. By the end of the 1930s, there were over seven million union members and unions had been established in most industries. These unions were to become very powerful in the USA after the war.

SOURCE 4 The 'Memorial Day Massacre' at the Republic steel plant in Chicago, 31 May 1937

SOURCE 5 Eyewitness interview (many years later), from Studs Terkel, *Hard Times*, 1970

❝ *General Motors refused to recognize the Union of Auto Workers (UAW). So at Christmas 1936, the workers at the General Motors plant in Flint, Michigan, staged a sit-in.*

The soup kitchen was outside the plant . . . ten to twenty women washing dishes and peeling potatoes in the strike kitchen. Mostly stews, pretty good meals, they were put in containers and hoisted up through the windows. The boys in there had their own plates and cups and saucers. . . .

The Company tried to shut off the heat. It was a bluff. Nobody moved for half an hour, so they turned them on again . . . The men sat in there for forty-four days . . . Then Mr Knudsen (head of General Motors) put his name to a piece of paper and says that General Motors recognizes the UAW . . . Until that moment, we were non-people. We didn't even exist. That was the big one. ❞

1. What do Sources 1–3 and 5 show about the methods and tactics used by employers to break strikes and prevent workers joining unions?
2. Why do you think the struggle was so violent?
3. Why were sit-ins like the one in Source 5 an effective weapon against employers?
4. How did the New Deal help the labour union movement?
5. a) What seems to have happened/be happening in Sources 3 and 4?
   b) Who might publish these pictures and why?
   c) In what ways could these give you a misleading impression of what was going on?
6. The sources on these pages present one version of the history of the struggle of the labour unions in the 1930s.
   a) How do you think the employers' version might be different?
   b) What photographs and written evidence might they produce to support their version?

Summing up the New Deal's success

■ REVIEW TASK

How successful was the New Deal? To answer this question you need to look back over the section on the New Deal from pages 101–105 as well as using information from pages 116–121. Copy and complete the grid below to help you do this task. Your teacher may be able to give you a copy to fill in.

Aim	Success			Failure	
	+2	+1	0	-1	-2
Bring government 'action, and action now'					
Put people back to work					
Restore confidence in banks					
Stop more businesses collapsing					
Help the poor					
Increase wages of people in work					
Restore farmers' incomes					
Help the Tennessee Valley and stop further soil erosion					
Help all Americans					
Restore Americans' faith in themselves					
Improve relations between bosses and workers					
Revive the American economy					
Make America a better place for ordinary people					

■ ACTIVITY

Use the chart above to help you write an essay entitled: How successful was the New Deal?

Try to reach a balanced judgement: explain how it was successful in some ways for some people, but not successful in other ways for other people. Add your own conclusions at the end, weighing up all the points.

Was Franklin D. Roosevelt good for America in the 1930s?

ROOSEVELT DIED IN April 1945, after he had led America successfully through most of the Second World War, helping to bring about the eventual defeat of Germany and Japan. This puts him among the all-time greats of this century and therefore colours any assessment of his achievements during the 1930s.

Would he have come out so well if he were judged at the end of the 1930s? Some people thought that he had made the central government too powerful and crushed 'rugged individualism' and self-reliance – qualities that had made America great. Others believed that he had prevented America from falling into the violence and chaos that had led to the rise of FASCISM in Europe.

Some of the points that historians have made for and against Roosevelt are set out below. Examine these points and the other evidence in this section to reach your own conclusions.

For

- He was the driving force behind the New Deal which left much of lasting value to America – roads, schools, public buildings, etc.
- He relieved the suffering of millions of Americans, by organising government-funded relief to prevent starvation and homelessness.
- He rescued the banking system and saved many businesses from collapsing, which stopped the situation in 1933 from becoming worse.
- He raised morale and inspired hope which gave the American people the courage to face the Depression and then meet the challenge of the Second World War.
- He saved democracy in America.

Against

- He did not get the American economy out of the Depression and his policies did not beat high unemployment.
- He did not do enough for certain groups, especially black people.
- He made the central government and the presidency too powerful, damaging the Constitution, especially the independence of the Supreme Court.
- He interfered too much in people's lives, taking away their self-reliance, e.g. by introducing social security.
- He prevented business from recovering as quickly as it might have done by creating so many rules and regulations, and helping the growth of powerful labour unions.

SOURCE 1 Hugh Brogan, *The New Deal,*

❝ To [his enemies] Roosevelt was a dangerous revolutionary who cut at the root of American liberty, justice and sacred property; a dictator who overthrew the ancient Constitution . . . ❞

SOURCE 2 Herbert Hoover, *The Memoirs of Herbert Hoover,* 1953

❝ [Under Roosevelt] we witnessed great centralization of power with a huge bureaucracy. We began a vast increase in government expenditure. We saw Congress reduced to a rubber stamp, and the Supreme Court subjugated . . .

As a result of eight years of the New Deal, there was not more but less liberty in America. And . . . we had not ended the Great Depression. Its vast unemployment and its huge numbers on relief were only ended by war. ❞

SOURCE 3 'The Industrial Giant', a cartoon about Roosevelt's New Deal

SOURCE 4 A.B. Lancaster, *The Americas,* 1984

❝ Others see as Roosevelt's major achievement his success in steering a liberal middle way between revolution and stagnation, between the political extremes of right and left . . . Above all, the USA under Roosevelt's New Deal had met the challenges of world depression without recourse to excesses of DICTATORSHIP experienced by so many millions in Europe during the same years. ❞

1. Why do Roosevelt's opponents in Sources 1 and 2 think he was bad for America? Mention at least three points.
2. What evidence can you find to support their views?
3. a) Why might you be careful about accepting Herbert Hoover's judgement in Source 2?
   b) Pick out any points where you think he is exaggerating his case.
4. What does the cartoon (Source 3) suggest about the way Roosevelt controlled the country?
5. Why does the writer of Source 4 believe Roosevelt saved the USA?

SOURCE 5 W. E. Leuchtenburg, *Franklin D. Roosevelt and the New Deal,* 1963

❝ Roosevelt's importance lay . . . in his ability to arouse the country and, more specifically, the men who served under him, by his breezy encouragement of experimentation, by his hopefulness, and . . . by his idealism. ❞

SOURCE 6 C.P. Hill, *The USA Since the First World War*, 1967

66 The legacy of the New Deal was in ideas and attitudes. These years brought a revolution in the thinking of the American people about the place of federal government in their lives ... The great reforms – the regulation of banking, the limitation upon hours of work – have remained part of the American social fabric, unchanged even in the years of Republican rule in the 1950s ...

It was not the least of Roosevelt's achievements that he gave new heart and new vigour to his fellow-countrymen just in time to face the trial of the Second World War. 99

6. How do the writers of Sources 5 and 6 sum up Roosevelt's contribution?

7. a) What aspect of Roosevelt's relationship with the American people does the cartoonist in Source 7 draw attention to?

b) Why was this so important in the 1930s?

SOURCE 7 'A man talking to his friends', a cartoon from an American newspaper, 1933

■ ACTIVITY

Roosevelt's death in 1945 meant that he was hailed as a great war leader who had protected the Free World from fascism. Imagine, however, that Roosevelt had died before America entered the war. How would people have viewed him then?

Write an OBITUARY for Roosevelt in 1939. Your obituary should be written from the viewpoint of one of the following:

■ a supporter of Roosevelt who believes his policies have been successful

■ an opponent who thinks Roosevelt has damaged the free spirit of America

■ a person who supported Roosevelt's New Deal but thinks that some of his measures had flaws and weaknesses. They did not agree with Roosevelt's plans for the Supreme Court.

Mention:

■ Roosevelt's background
■ his 1932 election campaign
■ Roosevelt's first 100 days as President
■ the Second New Deal
■ Roosevelt's battle with the Supreme Court
■ how successful/unsuccessful the New Deal measures were.

You will find information for your obituary by looking back through pages 99–125.

Why study the USA 1919–1941?

Here are four reasons for studying the USA between 1919 and 1941.

1. It helps you understand twentieth-century world history

- The USA has been the world's richest and most powerful country for most of the twentieth century. It dominates international politics and has a tremendous influence on the culture of countries throughout the world, not least Britain. We only have to mention the Hollywood film industry and American music to see how much it has affected, and still affects, our culture and our own lives today.
- The USA often undergoes changes which then happen in Britain and other countries, so studying them helps us understand our own history.
- The USA between the wars also contains people who are central characters in this century – Henry Ford, Al Capone and Franklin D. Roosevelt – and it's valuable to know more about these people and the circumstances in which they became important.

2. It helps you understand issues which are important today

- When millions of Europeans emigrated to the USA, they believed they were going to the land of opportunity and the 'land of the free'. You are now in a position to judge how far this was true. How free was American society for immigrants and black people in the 1920s and 1930s? What opportunities did they have? The issue of opportunities for minority groups in the USA is still hotly debated today.
- You have also seen how individual freedom versus government control was an important issue in the 1930s. When President Roosevelt brought in all the measures of the New Deal, some Americans called him a dictator. Today right-wing militia groups in the USA say they are fighting for freedom from excessive government control. Their white supremacist views are not very different from the ones you have read about in the early 1920s. In Britain too we have a continuing debate about how far the government should control our personal freedom. What are your views?

3. It helps you develop your source-handling skills

- Much of what we know or think we know about America in the 1920s and 1930s comes from films and television. This depth study has given you a chance to look at the evidence behind some of the images portrayed in the media. You have used eye-witness accounts, novels, photographs, tables, graphs, paintings and a wide range of other sources to reach you own conclusions. As well as learning about the USA, you will have developed useful skills.

4. It helps you learn lessons from history

- In the 1930s in Germany, economic chaos and violence, following the onset of the Great Depression, persuaded the German people to accept Adolf Hitler as their leader with the consequences that we know well. In America there was also economic chaos and violence, but the American people elected Franklin D. Roosevelt who steered the country through a difficult time and kept democracy alive. There are important lessons in the way he managed to do this. As a result, America was not overtaken by fascism. But what would happen if similar circumstances arose again?
- The 1929 Wall Street Crash, which turned into the Great Depression, taught the world an economic lesson about producing too many goods and gambling on the stock exchange. But has this lesson been learnt? The experience of Prohibition showed how dangerous it was to ban alcohol when the public wished to drink. Has this any similarities to the issue of drug taking today?
- So what do you think? What is the most useful thing you have learnt from your study of the USA between 1919 and 1941?

Glossary

anarchists people who believe that countries should not be ruled by organised governments, but by a system where everyone rules themselves through voluntary co-operation

Bootleggers manufacturers or suppliers of illegal alcohol

Brain Trust the group of experts who helped Roosevelt draw up the measures which formed the New Deal

Bolshevik Revolution In November 1917 the Bolsheviks seized political power and set up the world's first communist state

communism a system of government introduced in Russia after the Bolshevik Revolution of 1917. Its key features were state ownership of industry and agriculture, and strong central control of people's lives. It was based on the ideas of Karl Marx that eventually communism would develop so that there was no need for a government to rule people; instead everybody would work in co-operation with each other

Congress The law-making body of central government, made up of two elected houses: the House of Representatives and the Senate. Congress has power over foreign policy, taxation, defence, trade and currency

Constitution a set of rules which lay down how a country should be governed. It guarantees certain rights and freedoms to the people and puts limits on government power

Democracy a system of government where people have a say in how the country is run; elections are held between different political parties; people are free to express their opposition to the elected government

Democrats one of the two main political parties in the USA. Democrats are more likely to believe in intervention by the federal government to regulate industry and business; they favour measures to improve health, welfare and education

dictatorship a system of government where a strong leader has all the power. There are no elections so the dictator cannot be voted out of power and political opposition is not allowed

dries people who did not drink alcohol and supported the introduction of Prohibition

economic planning the management and control of the economy by central government

fanatics people whose enthusiasm or belief in something is beyond normal limits. They are prepared to commit extreme acts to help the cause they believe in

fascism the system of government introduced by Mussolini in Italy in the 1920s. Nazi Germany was also a fascist state from 1933–45. Key features: the country is ruled by a dictator, no elections, state control of the economy, and of people's behaviour and their ideas.

federal government the central government of the USA, based in Washington

flapper a young liberated woman from the 1920s. They dressed in the new fashions and did not behave in a traditional way

fundamentalists people of any religion who believe that events described in their holy books, e.g. the Bible, are literally true and should not be questioned

ghettos an area of a city where members of a particular ethnic or social group are forced or choose to live

Great Depression the period 1929-41 in the USA, which saw the crash of the stock market, thousands of businesses and banks going bankrupt, and high unemployment

immigrants people who leave their own country to settle permanently in another one

isolationism a policy of deliberately staying out of world affairs

laissez faire a policy of non-interference by government or other authorities; it literally means 'leaving things to sort themselves out'

mass-market market in which large numbers of people buy huge quantities of mass-produced goods

mass-production making large quantities of a product by using a standardised mechanical process or assembly line

modernists people who believe that religious teaching should be brought into line with modern views; for example, science has shown that the world developed over millions of years, rather than being made in seven days as the Bible says

obituary an account of the life of someone who has recently died

Pan-African the idea that there are cultural (and political) links between all black people who come from Africa or are of African descent. This means that black African Americans have a link with black Africans and share a common identity and heritage

pogrom organised persecution of Jews

Prohibition the 18th Amendment to the Constitution, which made the manufacture and sale of alcohol illegal in the USA 1920–33

radical a term that describes extreme political views. It can also mean a person or group who hold these views

refugees people who have been forced to leave their homes because of war or persecution

relief financial and other support from the government to help the hungry, homeless and unemployed

Renaissance a period in which art and literature flourish

repatriation people returning to their original homeland. The descendants of most black Americans had been forcibly taken from Africa to be sold as slaves

Republicans one of the two main political parties in the USA. Traditionally, Republicans have believed that the powers of the federal government should be limited and taxes should be kept down; they support policies that favour business and commerce, and dislike government-organised welfare schemes

reservations areas of land put aside for native American Indians. Many Indians were forced to live on these reservations because their traditional way of life had been destroyed

revues live entertainment provided by short sketches and songs

rugged individualism people overcoming problems and succeeding by their own efforts and hard work; not receiving help from the government

segregation laws which enforced the separation of black and white people in every aspect of life

self-indulgence enjoying pleasure, entertainment and an easy life

self-reliance relying on one's own hard work and success to make a living, and not expecting help or support from the government or other authorities

sharecroppers farmers who did not own the land they worked on. They were allowed to keep a share of the crops they grew, instead of receiving wages

speculation buying and selling stocks and shares in the hope of making a profit

stock market the place where stocks and shares are bought and sold

Supreme Court the highest court of law in the USA. It has the power to overturn decisions by all other courts and to decide whether new laws are constitutional

tariff a tax on foreign goods coming into a country

WASPs this stands for White Anglo-Saxon Protestants in the USA. They were the descendants of the earliest European immigrants who came mainly from Britain, Germany and Scandinavia

wet against the introduction of Prohibition

white supremacy the belief that white people are superior to all other races

Index

speakeasies 60
sport 25, 36
state government 13
Statue of Liberty 4, 8
steel industry 22, 35, 120
Steinbeck, John: *Grapes of Wrath* 76, 82, 83–4
strikes 17, 35, 44, 91, 120
St Valentine's Day Massacre 62, 64, 65
Supreme Court 12, 114

Temperance Movement 58
textile industry 35
Townsend, Doctor Francis 112
trade unions 70, 103, 105, 110
    opposition to 20–21, 32, 35, 44
transport industry 23, 24, 74; *see also* car industry
TVA (Tennessee Valley Administration) 104, 110

UAW (Union of Auto Workers) 121
unemployment 21, 112, 116
    Great Depression 73, 74, 75, 77, 78
    1920s 34
    First World War and 17
UNIA (Universal Negro Improvement and Conservation
    Association) 54, 55

Valentino, Rudolf 38
Vanzetti, Bartolomeo 47–9

wages 17, 21, 30, 34, 35, 40, 74
Wagner Act (1935) 105, 114, 120
Wall Street Crash 68–9
    causes of 70–71
Wall Street Stock Exchange 20, 68–9
WASPs (White Anglo-Saxon Protestants) 10, 50
WCFA (World Christian Fundamentalist Association) 57
Wilson, Woodrow 14, 17
women
    changing role of 40–43
    New Deal and 119
Women's Christian Temperance Union 58
working conditions 35, 44, 103
WPA (Works Progress Administration) 105, 110, 117
Wright, Richard 53, 54